Detours

TONY EVANS

Detours

The Unpredictable Path To Your Destiny

B&H
PUBLISHING GROUP
NASHVILLE, TENNESSEE

978-1-4336-8659-7

Published by B&H Publishing Group
Nashville, Tennessee

Dewey Decimal Classification: 234.9
Subject Heading: CHANGE (PSYCHOLOGY) \ FATE AND
FATALISM \ PREDESTINATION

3 4 5 6 7 8 9 10 • 21 20 19 18 17

ACKNOWLEDGMENTS

Thank you to the entire B&H Publishing Group team. First, to Jennifer Lyell who leads the trade books team so well and has believed in *Detours* from the start. To Devin Maddox, Kim Stanford, Dave Schroeder, and the countless others who brought together the many details required to create books out of words on a page—thank you. And to all of our LifeWay family, led by the courageous Thom Rainer, my sincerest gratitude extends out to you in Nashville, Tennessee. Thank you for your kingdom work.

CONTENTS

INTRODUCTION: What Is Destiny? 1

CHAPTER ONE: The Purpose of Detours 17

CHAPTER TWO: The Pain of Detours 27

CHAPTER THREE: The Pattern of Detours 41

CHAPTER FOUR: The Purifying of Detours 51

CHAPTER FIVE: The Proof of Detours 63

CHAPTER SIX: The Presence of Detours 73

CHAPTER SEVEN: The Promotion of Detours 83

CHAPTER EIGHT: The Plan of Detours 93

CHAPTER NINE: The Pardon of Detours 103

CHAPTER TEN: The Pleasure of Detours 113

CHAPTER ELEVEN: The Providence of Detours 125

CHAPTER TWELVE: The Perfection of Detours 135

CHAPTER THIRTEEN: The Perspective of Detours   145

CHAPTER FOURTEEN: The Peace of Detours   155

CHAPTER FIFTEEN: The Patience of Detours   165

CHAPTER SIXTEEN: The Path of Detours   177

CONCLUSION   191

APPENDIX: The Urban Alternative   201

What Is Destiny?

 Millions of people loved the television show *Seinfeld* when it aired. A college drama department did a study to find out why *Seinfeld* was so popular. They determined that the reason was because of its plotless programming. Seinfeld just meandered haplessly from one scene, one circumstance to the next without connection. The drama department concluded that Americans who lead plotless lives prefer plotless TV programs.

There's a plotlessness that exists in many of our lives today. Often we move from one scene, one circumstance, to the next without purpose. We wander from high school to college, from college to our first job. Then we're just dying to get married. Then we're just dying to have kids. Next we're dying to get them out of the house. Then we're dying to retire, only to find out that we're just dying—never having known why we were alive in the first place.

But what would life look like if we all lived with a purpose, with a destiny? How would we act and think differently if we saw God's hand in the plots of our lives connecting one circumstance to the next in the tapestry of His will? How would that affect our emotions? How would that affect our choices? How would that affect our outlook?

I believe it would affect it greatly because when you add purpose to the mix of pain and patience, it gives you the ability to push on. It gives you the ability to keep going when your get-up-and-go has gotten up and gone. It gives you the strength to accept and face your fears, disappointments, and pain rather than seek distractions to avoid them.

> Destiny *is the customized life calling for which God has equipped and ordained us, in order to bring Him the greatest glory and the maximum expansion of His kingdom.*

Since this book is called *Detours*—sharing biblical principles of how God will often take you from you where you are now to where He wants you to go—I thought it would be best if we started with a look at the destination. Let's look at what *destiny* means.

Destiny is *the customized life calling for which God has equipped and ordained us, in order to bring Him the greatest glory and the maximum expansion of His kingdom.* Every believer must understand first and foremost that his or her premiere destiny is to glorify God and make His name known (Isa. 43:6–7). Destiny always starts there. It always involves bringing glory to God somehow. It begins with the place of God integrating in our lives in such a way that people come into contact with Him through our words, spirit, emotions, or actions. If you want to find your destiny, find God. After all, He is the author of it.

And I don't mean "find Him" as if He's lost and you do not know Him. I mean get close to Him. Get to know God's heart. Come to recognize His voice more than anyone else's in your life. Learn what pleases Him and makes Him smile about you. Spend time with Him. Talk to Him. God must occupy the central place in your heart, mind, motivation, and actions (Deut. 6:5). After all, the heart of destiny itself is to serve the purposes of God.

As you obey and serve the Lord, He will make His purpose for you crystal clear (Prov. 3:5–7). You won't have to hunt for it, or chase it, or put out fleece upon fleece upon fleece to discern it. God is not playing hide-and-seek with your destiny. He just wants you to seek Him first, and then all of the things you need in your life will be given to you.

Why is finding and living out your destiny so important?

I have served as a pastor for more than forty years. This has given me the unique opportunity to be in people's lives at a level most do not experience. With that, I'm able to notice patterns that pop up routinely. One pattern I have seen repeatedly is this pattern of purpose linked to personal satisfaction. When people don't live with the sense that God has given them a divine purpose in life—or that they are fulfilling it—they become depressed. I've witnessed that more times than I wish. That's why I'm so passionate about helping people find the principles that can open up the path of destiny in their lives. Everyone has a destiny and a purpose to fulfill. Everyone.

Each member of the body of Christ has a unique role to play. But when some members don't fulfill their God-given destiny, the body cannot function (Rom. 12:4–8) as it was designed to function. Others are affected negatively when you do not live out your purpose. We are all interconnected in God's kingdom, and that's why it's critical that we all make seeking God and living out our purpose an important thing to do. Not just for others but also because it will benefit you.

When you discover your destiny, you'll begin to live life like you never have before. You will have skills to bounce back from disappointments and challenges, even pain. You will find resolve and determination that will enable you to accomplish things you didn't even know you could accomplish. Your passion and delight in what you do will be contagious to those around you, making your sphere of influence better as a result. You will push through things that used to defeat you.

Though persecution plagued the apostle Paul throughout his life, he frequently looked back to the destiny Jesus gave him on the Damascus Road and regained the confidence to keep going (Acts 9:3–6; 22:6–10). We know that we are fulfilling our purpose by the strength we find to keep going when circumstances say most people would give up.

Uniquely You

There was a little girl once who asked her father for a nickel. He reached into his pocket, but he didn't have any change. So the father pulled out his wallet, and all he had was a twenty-dollar bill. His little girl had been a good girl so he said, "Sweetie, I don't have a nickel, but here's a twenty-dollar bill."

The little girl pouted and said, "But Daddy, I want a nickel." The father tried to explain how many nickels the twenty-dollar bill represented, but she didn't get it. Many of us are the same. We want a nickel when God wants to give us a twenty-dollar bill. We want our will so much that we miss out on God's perfect destiny for us—one that is worth much more than twenty dollars!

Far too many of us are missing out on a glorious destiny because we want what we want. We want a nickel. We want what we know. What we can see. But God knows we were created for so much more. He desires to teach us what that is if we will learn to let go of our own plans and our own will and seek Him first.

Too many Christians believe they are "off the shelf" people. When we walk into a clothing store, we can choose from a number of shirts, belts, dresses, and pairs of shoes. But before these clothing items made it to the store shelf, they were mass-produced in a large factory, likely with little attention to each individual shirt, belt, or sock. But God doesn't produce "off the shelf" people. Each person has been custom-designed by His loving, sovereign hand. The fact that each person's fingerprints are completely unique proves that God doesn't mass-produce people.

Part of living out your destiny comes in living out the uniqueness of you. God has uniquely designed you for His purposes. God has woven you together intricately and uniquely to bring Him glory, bless others, and expand His kingdom. Psalm 139:13–14 says, "For it was You who created my inward parts; You knit me together in my mother's womb. I will praise You because I have been remarkably and wonderfully made."

Another verse which speaks to your personal stamp is found in Ephesians 2:10 (NASB): "For we are His workmanship, created in Christ Jesus for good works, which God prepared beforehand so that we would walk in them." In this verse the word *workmanship* means "masterpiece." Keep in mind that the title *masterpiece* is reserved for the most glorious example of a certain art form, such as a poem, a painting, a sculpture, or a piece of music. Masterpieces are known as such because of the skill and expertise of their creator. Because of this, God's masterpieces must be set apart (1 Pet. 1:2–4). In order for you to be the masterpiece God wants you to be, He must sanctify you and make you more like Jesus Christ. To do this, He often puts detours in your life in order to develop you. He takes you on a path that will give you the grace to grow. God will continue shaping and molding you as His masterpiece over the course of many detours until you are ready to fully realize all He has for you to do.

Not only are you a masterpiece, but God has also prepared good works for you to do. That means the good works God has prepared for you are the biblically authorized activities that bring God glory and benefit others. As you walk in the path of good works He has laid out, you will fulfill your destiny. Sometimes this requires learning, growing, and developing as a person. These seasons are what we can refer to as a detour. They are times when God seeks to mold us into the character He can use for the good works He has prepared. That's not always fun. Sometimes it hurts. It's often longer than any of us wish. But God will accomplish His desired result, if you allow Him. It's only when we fuss, fight, and complain that our detours drag on longer than necessary.

When you iron a shirt that is wrinkled, you have to add steam and heat in order to get the wrinkles out. And why do we iron shirts, pants, and dresses? Because we want to look good when we wear them. In the same way, God has to put us through the fires of refinement to smooth out the rough places and correct our flaws.

Now imagine if that shirt you were ironing wouldn't sit still. Imagine if it kept hopping up off the ironing board. Or what if it would bundle itself up into a tight ball each time you attempted to iron it. How long would that ironing session take, then, if the shirt simply lay flat and allowed you to press it into perfection?

The same holds true for us on our detours. Far too often, we are the cause of our own delays. We are the cause of our own additional detours. Our lack of compliance with God's development in our hearts, spirit, and souls will far too often prolong that which we do not enjoy. Surrender is a critical secret to speeding up the process toward your destiny.

We, as God's masterpieces, bear our Master's name and image. He wants to make sure that image reflects Him well. When we fulfill our God-ordained destinies, God wants others to see the beauty of Him through us, and that takes refinement in us.

Tools of Destiny

A hammer and a chisel in the hands of a sculptor can turn a piece of stone into a work of art. With each blow, as the hammer strikes the chisel, chunks of stone fall away, eventually revealing a beautiful sculpture. Though the process of chipping away at the stone seems harsh and unyielding, the result is well worth the pain.

Likewise, when God gets His hands on our joyful and painful experiences, He can turn our lives into masterpieces that display His glory and channel His blessings to others. God will use our skills, training, and interests to help us discover our purpose in life.

He will also turn our failures and sin into opportunities to form us into the people He created us to be. And even when we face injustice, persecution, and unbearable tragedy, God will transform our pain into a passion for Him—if we let Him.

Some of the primary tools God uses to help us identify our divine-designed destinies are our experiences. God is able to thread together the good, the bad, and the bitter experiences life has taken us through to shape a beautiful masterpiece of destiny and to accomplish His purpose in our lives.

But you guessed it. You can't have experiences without going through—yes—experiences. Detours are often those opportunities God uses in our lives to chisel us through the experiences we face. We can either cooperate with these detours by asking God to reveal to us the lessons He wants us to learn, or the skills He wants us to develop—and so on, or we can complain, kick, scream, fight, and remain on the detour much longer than we ever needed to.

One of the things that can help you and me as we go through various experiences in life that we may not want to go through is to remember this biblical truth: God uses all of our experiences to bring Him glory, when we allow Him. God sovereignly works through all of our detours to glorify Himself and achieve what is best for our development and the good we are to bring to others (Rom. 8:28–30). Through good, bad, and bitter experiences, God prepares you to fulfill His plan.

The Good

Good experiences are the positive things that have happened as a result of God's will and your good choices. These might be your education, connections, family, accomplishments, and more. God will use them to craft you specially to fulfill His plan. This can happen even if you did not set out to serve God in these experiences you acquired. For example, God took Saul's training as a Pharisee, sanctified it, and used it to prepare the converted "Paul" to craft the theological foundation of the church in the New Testament letters he wrote (Acts 22:3).

God also used Peter's trade as a fisherman to turn him into a fisher of men and a leader in the early church (Matt. 4:18–20). God used Moses's training in the royal Egyptian household to give him access to redeem God's people (Exod. 3:10). God used Esther's beauty to make her the queen so she could save His people (Esther 4:14).

The Bad

God will also use your bad experiences to achieve His will. Bad experiences are the mistakes, sins, failures, consequences, and regrets that have occurred because of your own choices. God can take your bad experiences and turn them into tools to bring Him glory. For example, Peter denied Jesus three times, but God used that failure to humble Peter and prepare him for ministry and to strengthen other Christians (Luke 22:31–34).

How did God bring Peter back after he denied Jesus? When Peter was out fishing on the Sea of Galilee, he saw Jesus on the shore cooking fish over a charcoal fire. The Greek word for *charcoal* is only used two times in the New Testament—once when Peter was warming his hands over a charcoal fire when he denied Jesus, and the other time when Jesus cooked Peter's breakfast over the charcoal fire. God took Peter back to the place of his failure—to the charcoal fire where he denied his Lord—humbled him, and then told him to feed His sheep. Finally, Peter was ready to help others.

One thing to remember with regard to the bad experiences in your life is that you must learn from your failures and the consequences of bad choices and be humbled so God can use them for His good. God will often take you back to a point similar to that of a time of failure in your life to retest you, or to remind you—so that you can be humble and grow.

The Bitter

Last, God uses your bitter experiences to accomplish His desires. Bitter experiences are the things that have happened to you but that are not your fault, such as abandonment, abuse, neglect, injustice, and disease. As we will study in our time together in this book on detours, Joseph was born into a dysfunctional family, sold by his brothers, wrongly accused by Potiphar's wife, sent to jail unjustly, and forgotten. No story quite spells bitter like Joseph's.

Yet in His perfect timing, God elevated Joseph to a position of influence. Joseph didn't allow bitterness to take over from negative experiences that he clearly did not deserve. Rather, he saw God's hand working through evil people and injustice to put him in a position to save his family and his people (Gen. 50:20). As Joseph recognized God's sovereignty, he trusted Him and didn't allow bitterness to take root in his heart (Gen. 39:20–23).

Some of the primary things God uses to help us identify His divine, designed destiny are our good, bad, and bitter experiences. God has the ability to take our mess, or the mess people mess over us with, and construct our miracles. Yet one of the reasons many people stay stuck on detour after detour after detour is they have not learned from their failures, or they have not learned to forgive other people's failures.

God has a way of taking bad and making it better when we surrender to His hand, His sovereignty, His plan.

It's All about Alignment

Just like a car must be in alignment in order to drive smoothly down the roads of life, we also need to be spiritually aligned with God in order to travel our journey smoothly. Doors remain closed when we are out of alignment. Detours remain looming for miles and miles up ahead. Alignment is one of those critical spiritual components that so few people seem to fail to grasp, and even more fail to apply. Yet it can open up your pathway to destiny faster than almost anything else (John 15:5).

There was a businessman who had a demanding day ahead of him and was already late for work. He turned on the car, put it in reverse, and punched the button on the garage door opener. Nothing happened. He hit it again and again, a little harder each time. Still nothing. *I've got to get out of this garage and make it to work in time for my big meeting*, he thought. Frustrated, he put the car in park, pulled out his cell phone, and called the garage door repairman.

When the repairman answered the phone, the businessman explained the situation and begged for help. "I can't get to my destination because I'm stuck in my garage."

The garage door repairman told the businessman to walk over to the garage door and find what looked like canisters at the bottom left and bottom right of the door. So the businessman found the canisters.

The repairman asked, "Are the red lights at the center of the canisters pointed exactly at each other?" The businessman noticed that the red lights in one of the canisters were not in alignment.

The repairman said, "That's your problem. When the red lights are not in perfect alignment, the door can't receive the signal to open." After the businessman shifted the canister a little bit, the red lights matched up, the door opened, and he was off to tackle his busy day.

One of the reasons people have trouble staying on detours too long is because they are out of alignment with God—the only one who can give them the straight line ahead. If Christians live misaligned lives, we won't get His signal. We won't hear "Turn here," when we need to. Or "talk to this person," or "apply for this job." Rather, we will be stuck trying to constantly figure things out on our own based on logic and reasoning. While logic and reasoning have their place, far too many unknowns exist on the path of life—things we can't see, hear, or even predict may happen. Only God knows the beginning from the end. Only God knows what He has planned down the road. Logic and reasoning can only discern within the context of their own awareness. But when you are aligned with God and abiding in His Spirit, He will guide your spirit like a personal GPS system.

Many people who have a TV have a satellite dish of some sort. When the dish picks up the frequency, you get a picture and you can see your favorite TV show clearly. But when the signal is interrupted, though the signal has been sent, your dish doesn't pick it up. And you can't see anything on your TV.

Likewise, God wants to give you the next steps on your detours to your destiny. But He wants to know that you're in a place to receive His message. That means you must remove yourself from the static of this world order, from thoughts that deny the spiritual framework of biblical truth—from materialism, distraction, and worldliness.

When you abide in His presence, He speaks.

The Lord spoke to the apostles and set Paul and Barnabas apart for His purpose *while* the apostles were worshipping the Lord in His presence (Acts 13:2–3). God often gives us guidance as we practice spiritual disciplines, including worship, fasting, and prayer. What is worship? Worship is positioning your spirit in alignment with God so you can hear from Him. When you worship God, you acknowledge who He is, what He has done, and what you trust Him to do in the future. You acknowledge and rest in His preeminence over all, even yourself. The Lord wants to give you guidance, but you must remain in a position to hear Him.

If you feel you are out of alignment, one thing you can do is begin living in submission to Him. Scripture says this is our daily act of worship. Sacrificing your perspective, plans, and will for His aligns your soul with Him. Then you are able to understand His perfect will and see His will being worked out in your life (Rom. 12:1–2).

When a baby is breach, her head is up. The doctor has to go in and turn the baby around and point the little head down. But when her head is in the right place, it's time for a delivery.

When you live with your mind and thoughts focused in the wrong direction, you will have a difficult time finding your destiny. You will go on detour after detour after detour. But when you allow the Great Physician to turn you around—to bow your head down, even though the process may feel painful, you become ready to walk with purpose.

Always remember, even in the dark places, God has a plan for you. The good news is you don't have to find the exit of your detours yourself. You just have to find God, and He will give you your exit ramp. But before He does, He may have a few things to prepare first. Let's learn about those in the next chapters.

CHAPTER ONE

The Purpose of Detours

 Detours are delays. They are rerouted paths that keep us from our original route. Detours pop up in places we had not expected. When we get in our cars, we do so with a destination in mind. We plan to go *somewhere*.

And we typically know *how* we plan to get there—which highway we are going to take, which turn to avoid rush-hour traffic, and which side streets we are going to use to arrive at our final destination.

And even if we don't know the way, we can type the destination address into our smartphone app, and rely on an automated voice to guide us through every turn.

Regardless if we are following our own mental map or the voice in our phone, sometimes we run into a detour (something we did not expect). Some roadblock that requires us to make a U-turn or go down a path we did not expect.

I don't know about you, but I like to get to where I am going without any detours.

In fact, when the kids were younger and we loaded them all into the car to drive from Dallas to Baltimore to visit my parents each summer, I barely even stopped. Sometimes I would race myself based on the last year's time clock in order to see if I could beat my previous time.

If the kids needed to use the bathroom, I told them to wait. If they were thirsty, they had to wait. There was a method to my madness, you see. If I got the kids a drink, then we would have to stop more down the road to use the bathroom. Essentially, they all buckled down at my mercy because I had a destination at which to arrive.

As you might imagine, if I won't even stop for normal things like food and bathroom breaks, you can guess how I feel about a detour. It's not good.

I sigh.

I moan.

I wonder why on earth did this have to happen to me right now.

Have you ever done something similar? Have you ever been driving down the road when all was well only to arrive at a construction site with orange signs and arrows and experience your whole attitude and outlook change?

I've admitted that mine changed; you can admit it too.

Detours are typically unexpected inconveniences that, without fail, cause a speed bump in your emotions. It's either a sign you come up on, or a person who steers you elsewhere, or a police car with lights on it sitting there to let you know the road you are traveling is no longer available. Now, because of the detour, you and I must go off the beaten path, take longer than we had wished to, and be inconvenienced in order to arrive where we had hoped to go.

Few of us like to be stalled for any reason. Even if it's just someone cutting us off in traffic and forcing us to slow down. But detours are necessary if any improvement is going to be made on the paths we travel. Or if any wreck is going to be cleaned up or hazard avoided. Detours are designed for our own good, regardless of how we view or feel about them. Detours are good things that often feel bad.

Divinely designed detours are positive interruptions designed to divert down a better path so that we might have the opportunity to reach our destination at all.

> *Detours are good things that often feel bad.*

Let me repeat that since it is something we don't often hear: *Detours can be a good thing*. They provide safety, opportunities for road improvement, and a different way to get where we want to go.

If you were to sit at a detour sign and stubbornly refuse to take the diversion, you would go nowhere. You would just sit there. For days. Possibly weeks sometimes.

Yes, a detour may take longer than you had originally planned; however, it won't take any longer than if you were to try to push through it on the original path. That will get you nowhere.

Detours on the Road of Life

If you are a believer in Jesus Christ, you have a destination. We often refer to that throughout this book, and in life, as your *destiny*.

From an eternal perspective, we know what our destiny is to be and that it involves being in God's presence forever—worshipping Him and working for Him in our eternal state. That is our *eternal destiny*.

But each of us also has a time-bound destiny here on Earth. I call this our *historical destiny*. It is the unique purpose you and I have been created for in order to fulfill.

God has a plan for you. He has a plan for your life. He has a purpose for your existence. The reason why you were not taken to heaven the moment after you were converted is because there is a purpose on the earth; He desires you to live out your destiny. Your destiny is not just to go through the motions day-in and day-out. It is a God-designed stamp on your soul that involves the use of your time, talents, and treasures for His glory and other people's good for the advancement of His kingdom. As you fulfill your destiny, you receive the satisfaction and contentment that come from living out your calling. You receive the peace that come from purpose.

Rarely though does God ever take someone to their destiny without taking them on at least one detour, or two, or ten, or one hundred. It is the one-in-a-million Christian who gets to go from point A to B to C and straight on to Z. Most often, God takes you from A to F to D to R to B to Q, and so on. You never know which letter He is pulling you toward next.

As people, we like to plan. We make our itineraries when we travel. We keep a log of our schedule on a calendar app. We appreciate the efficiency of moving forward steadily. We would never plan chaos and detours into our life on purpose. And yet that seems to be God's *modus operandi*—His default mode for guiding us.

This is because it is in our detours that we become developed for our destiny.

Development

Part of experiencing the fullness of your destiny is in understanding your detours. Far too often we fail to understand our detours, and as a result, we wind up viewing them in a wrong light. When this happens, we give room for things like impatience, bitterness, regret, and doubt to grow. Rather than allowing the detours to produce the development we need, they actually set us back spiritually, thus setting us up with a need for more detours in order to grow. It can become a vicious cycle.

For example, when you were in school, you would have to endure academic testing. These tests let the teacher know where you stood on the material you needed to learn. If you were unable to pass these tests, then more assignments and more tests would have to be given. Have you ever known someone who "tested out" of a class or an assignment? This happened when they felt they had enough knowledge to pass the test without having to do the work. In this case, they took a test and if they scored high enough, they could skip the rest of the course.

I never "tested out" of a course, but I know people who did. Most of us have to go through the learning process—unfortunately, some of us more often than others—in order to gain mastery over what we need to know.

God is not going to bring your destiny to fruition until He knows you are able to handle it spiritually, emotionally, and physically. If you cannot handle it, you will *lose it* rather than *use it*, for His glory. That is why He focuses so intently on our development as He takes us to our destiny.

When you look at Scripture, it is full of destinies being reached by detour. When God told Israel He would take them to their destiny in Canaan, they had to cross the Red Sea in order to get there. However, He didn't take them directly to the Red Sea. Rather, He took them down south and then brought them back up before He led them across the Red Sea. In fact, because they had not yet developed in their level of faith that they needed in order to conquer the enemy in the Promised Land, they wound up wandering on a forty-year detour before ever reaching their destiny.

The timing and length of our detours in life are often dependent upon our personal choices and growth. God may have a short detour planned for us, but sometimes through our hardheadedness, stubbornness, or immaturity God extends our detour.

Moses was on a detour for forty years. He knew what God wanted him to do. God wanted him to deliver his people from slavery. Yet it took forty years in the wilderness to develop Moses into the humble and trusting servant he needed to be in order to have the mind-set, faith, and abilities to carry out the plan.

Abraham was on a twenty-five-year detour. At one point God had told him His plan for him—that He would bless nations through Abraham and make his name great. How could Abraham have thought at that time it would be twenty-five years before he would have a son? The vision and the proclamation from God to Abraham were real and vivid. It would have been odd for Abraham to believe at that point that it would be nearly three decades before he would witness the literal birth of it.

When we give a plan or projection to someone, we typically do so shortly before we plan to carry it out. Yet God is not like us and will often give us a glimpse of our destiny long before we are prepared to actualize it, as He did when He told Abraham that there would be a four-hundred-year detour in Egypt before they would reach their promised destination (Gen. 15:12–16).

The greatest apostle in the New Testament, Paul, went on a three-year detour to a desert where God removed him from the front page of culture and life in order to strengthen him, teach him, and develop him for his calling.

I could go on and on with biblical examples of detours, but I think you get the picture. Detours are often a regular part of God's plan in guiding us to our destinies.

God *has* a destiny for you. He has a purpose and a place He wants you to live out. But it may not happen tomorrow. You probably won't get there by going in a straight line. Patience is the primary virtue needed in order to reach your destiny.

The following is a passage speaking on "trials," but we can easily substitute the word *affliction* with *detours* and arrive at the same intended meaning:

> And not only that, but we also rejoice in our afflictions *[detours]*, because we know that affliction *[detours]* produces endurance, endurance produces proven character, and proven character produces hope. This hope will not disappoint. (Rom. 5:3–5)

Hope does not disappoint. Detours disappoint momentarily. But when we allow them to produce hope, God promises that hope will not disappoint. And in order to arrive at an authentic hope in your spirit, accepting your detours is necessary.

Just as your muscles will not grow stronger simply by wishful thinking, the painful process of strengthening your hope comes by detours, afflictions, and trials. Show me someone with an indomitable hope, and we will see someone who has had his or her share of detours. I promise you this is true. Authentic hope is a learned trait.

Now, I don't mean wishful thinking or an optimistic attitude. I am referring to that level of hope that stays steady despite the storm and circumstances, which circle you in waves of chaos, testing, and pain.

Joseph's Detours

There is no person in Scripture who better illustrates the principles of detours in relationship to destiny than Joseph. His life reads like a good suspense novel; it displays like an epic film. It has twists and turns along the way. Not only that, it contains stories within stories within stories. If you didn't skip ahead to the end, you may wonder how it could ever end well along the way. But it does. Moving ahead from chapter 37 up to 50, we catch the culmination of the detours and distresses when it gives us Joseph's response to those who had served as the catalyst to his life's chaos. We read,

> But Joseph said to them, "Do not be afraid, for am I in God's place? As for you, you meant evil against me, but God meant it for good in order to bring about this present result, to preserve many people alive." (Gen. 50:19–20 NASB)

Please notice the phrase, "You meant evil against me, but God meant it for good." This insightful inclusion in Scripture gives us a clue as to the makeup of detours. They may oftentimes contain evil. They may oftentimes contain bad people. In fact, in our lives it can even be our own bad choices that set us off on a detour. In this cosmic battle of good against bad, we cannot expect to escape without coming in close contact with that which intends our harm.

Yet what we often do is stay stuck there. We suffer under the evil of people acting badly or our own bad choices producing bitterness, cynicism, hate, and stunted growth. It is only when we read the entire phrase—keeping in the part that Joseph included "but God meant it for good"—that we are able to move forward, grow, trust, and reach our destiny.

Bad and good happen concurrently in order to bring us to the place God has for you. The first and greatest lesson in detours includes recognizing this reality at a level that allows you to trust God and His hand in the midst of evil, sin, and disappointment in your life.

God is greater than all of it and will use it for good when we surrender to Him through a heart of faith, hope, forgiveness, and love.

CHAPTER TWO

The Pain of Detours

 I know what it is like to wait on a vision. Having been in ministry for more than four decades, I've had my fair share of the Lord giving me a dream I felt was from Him, only to have it derailed for lengths of time.

Even as I write this book, I am in the midst of one of these scenarios. It involves a piece of property God put on my heart to purchase more than a decade ago. It's a beautiful twenty-two-acre slice of heaven in the heart of south Dallas. An immaculate, colonial style home, built in the 1930s, sits on its pristine grounds. So beautiful is this home, it's been used as a setting in the film *Tender Mercies*.

I don't exactly know why, but when this property came on the market many years ago, my spirit wouldn't rest until I prayed through pursuing it. I knew it was mine. I knew it had a purpose. I couldn't see the purpose, but the Spirit wouldn't let me have peace until I acquired it.

Now purchasing twenty-two acres of tree-filled land, along with a house and pool, is no small decision. Especially when my wife and I still live in the same small, one-level home we have lived in for more than thirty-five years. It didn't make sense why I would pursue this property with our own personal finances rather than move my wife and me to a beautiful new home for the same price. After all, we weren't going to live on this property ourselves. But God made it plain to me that I needed to get it while it was available. And so—after praying and talking with Lois about it, and coming to an agreement that the Lord was putting it on our hearts to acquire it—we did.

Over the years, it has done many things. It has served as the location of our Crisis Pregnancy Center for our church. It has been a place for events and family outings. In fact, our granddaughter Kariss married her husband, Joshua, there not too long ago. But it wasn't until only recently when I realized what I had bought this property for so many years ago. At the time I got it, the vision for our legacy training center hadn't even been birthed. It wasn't even an embryo at that point. Because the concept had not yet been conceived, God could not tell me why I needed the property. He could only tell me that I needed it.

Since that original purchase date, I have aged into my legacy-planning years. During this time, our national ministry felt led of the Lord to launch a strategic online training program, along with localized courses, to codify my lifetime of learning. As we went through the planning stages for this training center, the twenty-two acres of land located just a stone's throw from our own home presented itself as the perfect location for these headquarters. It also gives us a wonderful and beautiful location for smaller retreat-type training events as I grow older and travel less.

God knew way back then what He wanted this land for now; and had I not acted in faith on His Spirit's prompting, it may not be available to us now. Sometimes God asks us to take the next step without showing us the destination. Living a life of faith involves detours. When we understand that this is a normative reality, we become more willing to take steps in faith while trusting that God will reveal the rationale and reason as time moves on.

A Dysfunctional Home

Joseph's story illustrates this better than nearly anything else I know. His story begins for us in the Bible when Joseph is seventeen years old. The eleventh son of Jacob, we discover Joseph as a teenager in a very dysfunctional home. His father is known as a deceiver and a trickster. All his life, Jacob deceived and tricked people in order to get his way. He was a manipulator by trade. One of the more infamous deceptions he is known for is tricking his father into giving him the birthright that was due to his older brother rather than him.

Jacob had twelve sons by four different women, which explains a lot of the dysfunction—twelve boys by four women can give rise to some serious complications down the line. In the midst of baby-mama drama, the children grew up to create various kinds of chaos. One of the sons, Reuben, had sex with one of his father's wives. When Jacob found out about it—which he did—you could imagine what happened. Reality TV has nothing on Joseph's family. You may be able to keep up with the Kardashians in our world today, but I doubt anyone could keep up with Joseph and his brothers. They would have been kicked off television simply due to the level of crisis they faced. Social media would have shut them down and got them kicked off the network.

Two of Joseph's brothers, Simeon and Levi, are mass murderers. In Genesis 34:25 we read, "On the third day, when they [the city's men] were still in pain, two of Jacob's sons, Simeon and Levi, Dinah's brothers, took their swords, went into the unsuspecting city, and killed every male." Not surprisingly, these two brothers set up the township for murder through deception. They talked the entire town into getting circumcised and then brutally rampaged while they were healing and unable to fight back.

Then there is Joseph's brother Judah who had sexual relations with his daughter-in-law. Holidays in Joseph's home would have been a disaster, no doubt. This is one messed-up family. If you or I were looking for a home out of which to pick the future savior of an entire nation—and even the known world to a large degree—from starvation by famine, it is doubtful we would have landed on

Jacob and his twelve sons. How could anything good come out of such mess?

Add on top of already volatile emotions the dynamics of favoritism, and you have a concoction worthy of a witch's brew. But in Genesis 37:3 we find just that, "Now Israel [Jacob] loved Joseph more than his other sons because Joseph was a son born to him in his old age, and he made a robe of many colors for him." This is the verse where we are introduced to the famous "coat of many colors" which Jacob gave Joseph, sparking a fury of jealousy in the family.

The reason Joseph was the favorite son when he was born as the eleventh was that his mother, Rachel, was the wife Jacob actually loved. He had worked seven years for her when he got tricked into having to marry her sister, Leah, instead. He then had to work another seven years for Rachel. Rachel gave birth to two sons, Joseph and Benjamin, before she died. She died when giving birth to Benjamin, so when Joseph was a teenager, Jacob favored Joseph above all others.

No one else got a special gift from their father, as far as we can tell. Joseph was the only one who received this unique multicolored piece of clothing. It was a status symbol in its own right. In 2 Samuel 13:18 we read about the royal robe the daughters of the king wore to indicate their royalty. We can compare it today to the robe you get when you are graduating from college. While it isn't an exact comparison, this gives you an idea of the robe's symbolism. It wasn't just a piece of new clothing; it meant something. It sent a message loud and clear to the rest of the entire family that Joseph was the most beloved. He was the chosen one of his father to occupy the privileged position that belonged to the eldest son.

As you might imagine, this made his family irritated, to say the least. We read, "When his brothers saw that their father loved him more than all his brothers, they hated him and could not bring themselves to speak peaceably to him" (Gen. 37:4). Joseph's brothers hated him so much they couldn't even speak kindly to him. These brothers understood that the robe meant much more than favoritism. It meant who their father was choosing to give the double portion of his blessing to. It communicated legacy, inheritance, and an exalted position, which is why he was placed as overseer and investigator of his brothers' work. It was, in short, a perfect storm for a family disaster.

Add to this storm the lightning and thunder of a dream, and you have a recipe for murder. Shortly after getting the robe, Joseph had a dream in which he saw his brothers bowing down to him as sheaves of grain. At the tender age of seventeen, Joseph didn't have the wisdom to keep that type of dream to himself. So when he told his brothers about what he saw, they mocked him and said, "'Are you really going to reign over us?' his brothers asked him. 'Are you really going to rule us?' So they hated him even more because of his dream and what he had said" (v. 8).

They already hated him just because of the coat of many colors. Pile the dream on top of that and they "hated him even more." But not only that, in verse 9 we discover Joseph has another dream. This time the sun, moon, and eleven stars bowed down to him.

When he told his father about this dream, his father rebuked him for thinking they would one day bow down to him. Joseph's dreams had even gone so far as to offend the one who loved him most. You can imagine what these dreams did to his brothers.

His brothers were done with him. Due to Joseph's God-given dream, the people around him were now so jealous of him that they could not stand to even be around him. Joseph's dreams would later go on to be proven true, but at the time he received them, the people around Joseph were not ready to hear them.

Sometimes this can happen with us, can't it? God can place a dream or a vision in our heart that may seem too big to those around us. If you share it with others, you may get naysayers who try to talk you out of believing it. Not every vision God gives you is intended for those around you to know. Their hearts may not yet be ready to see and believe your dream because God has not yet developed their understanding. Wisdom is the ability to know when and what to share. Just because the Lord lays something on your heart doesn't mean you should tell it to everyone.

Before he hit his eighteenth birthday, Joseph had made three critical mistakes. The first one we read about early on in the chapter where "[Joseph] brought back a bad report about them to their father" (Gen. 37:2). Joseph tattletaled on his brothers. The second mistake was sharing his dreams of ruling over his family with his family. The third mistake involved sporting his special coat, most likely in a way that wasn't very humble. He's a teenager. More than that, he's a teenager in a dysfunctional family. Most likely, he's an immature teenager at best. Joseph doesn't know how to accept favor correctly or transfer information to whom and when. Apparently he still has some things that need correcting in his character.

Cue detour number one.

The First Detour

As I mentioned in the last chapter, the purpose of detours is to develop you for the destiny God has for you. When God is ready to move you to the next spiritual level (toward your destiny), things may get worse before they get better. You may not like that statement, but that doesn't make it any less true.

When God is ready to move you to the next spiritual level (toward your destiny), things may get worse before they get better.

Development is often a painful process of breaking us of our own ambitions and independence so we can live a life of surrender and obedience before God. God creates detours in order to perform some construction on the pathways of our soul. He has to chip away at the parts that don't fit where He is taking us. He has to strengthen the things that aren't ready for our destiny just yet. And depending on how we respond to our detours, we may need to be roadblocked several times before we reach where we are supposed to go.

Development is always part of the process of destiny. God wants to make sure you are ready for your destiny before He brings you to it. There would be nothing worse than Him bringing you to your destiny, and you messing it up because you aren't able emotionally, spiritually, or even physically to handle it well. Timing is a key ingredient in God's recipe for your life.

I know so many of us have dreams of shiny lives and magnificent futures—love like in the movies, careers that satisfy us while affording us our greatest desires, and families that reflect our greatest hopes. Yet God says, "I can't put you where you need to be until I clean you up first." He cannot grant us our destiny if we will not allow Him to shape our character; God must deal with our sins, our flaws, our fears, doubts, and immaturity. Until God is free to produce and promote righteousness within us, He is not free to move us to our intended destination. We have to take a detour first, and second, third, and so on until we have been developed enough to handle what He has in store.

So few Christians understand that.

If we could only grasp this truth, it would make the way we view trials differently. If we could see the purpose through the pain, we would bear up under it with a great deal more dignity. But because we don't, we often wind up like Joseph—learning lessons of loss, lust, and lies. Over and over and over, *ad nauseum*.

Joseph's first lesson landed him in a pit. A literal pit. While shepherding the sheep with his brothers, his brothers came up with a scheme to put him to death. They saw the dreamer in the distance and decided to destroy his dream once and for all. So they threw him in a pit and decided to spin a tale that a wild beast had devoured him (v. 20).

Joseph's older brother Reuben spoke up and persuaded the brothers not to kill Joseph but to instead strip him of his colored coat and sell him instead. They stripped Joseph of what he valued most—his significance and sign of favor and royalty. This is also what happens to us sometimes. Have you ever noticed that the very thing you fear losing the most is often the thing you lose? We all have different personalities and different things we dread, but God knows until we are able to let go of what we prize the most, we will always place our desires and our will above His own. That's why He asked Abraham to sacrifice the most precious thing to him—his son—in the story of Abraham, Isaac, and the ram.

You may have experienced this at work. If you gave your time, passion, and dedication only to be overlooked for promotion or even let go prematurely, you know what it is like to lose something of value. Or perhaps you experienced this in the home. You served and loved your family for decades only to have your spouse leave you and your kids scarred by the breakup. Too many times we rely on ourselves until we get stripped of our own self-sufficiency. God will often let us hit rock bottom so we will discover that He is the rock at the bottom.

Joseph valued his position of royal favor in the family. So the Lord allowed his brothers to dethrone him by ripping off his coat and tossing him into a pit.

Joseph had *literally* hit rock bottom.

A pit is a hole you cannot get out of by yourself. It is a situation you cannot fix. It's a wayward or rebellious child you cannot control or convince to come back home.

It's a boss you cannot escape from.

Or a family member who is driving you into depression.

It's a mate who is unresponsive.

A pit is so many things, but mainly it is a situation in which you find yourself stuck. This is because when God takes you on a detour, you may often wind up at a roadblock first. Just sitting there stuck.

Joseph didn't dig the hole. He didn't create the pit. But he was in it.

With no water.

No food.

No energy.

No hope.

Maybe the dreamer even thought his dreams were now shattered. He heard his brothers whispering about whether or not they should kill him. He was at their mercy now. He had lost all control.

Sometimes God allows things to be out of control so we will learn that we never had control in the first place. Detours are divine interventions—usually even divine disappointments—where God intentionally addresses our character and matures us spiritually.

The greater the destiny, the deeper the detour—the pit.

Eventually some Ishmaelite traders came along the path, and Joseph's brothers opted to profit off of him rather than to kill him. So they killed an animal instead and put the animal's blood on Joseph's garment in order to lie to their father that he had died. Then they cashed in on some silver for selling their brother as a slave. One minute Joseph was living large; the next minute he's chained to a caravan marching slowly through a desert. A desert is not usually the place someone looks to find their destiny. But a desert is often a place God will bring each of us to in order to develop us for our own.

Stripped of his tunic. Ripped from his home. Dethroned from his dream. Joseph made his way to Egypt no doubt afraid and definitely alone. Not such a good setup for a future prince and ruler. But that's just like God. He loves us enough to mold us into the person He has designed us to be.

I can't imagine the pain God bears in witnessing our own, especially when we can't understand what He is doing. When we blame Him. Yell at Him. Ignore Him. Become bitter toward Him. And all along He knows what He is allowing is for our good, His glory, and the benefit of those we love. But He takes our punches and defends our blows because He knows that someday we will recognize His hand of kindness and direction and thank Him.

Friend, you may be in a bad place right now. You may be in a pit without water, food, or fellowship. You may feel like you are the only one in a perfect storm designed to take you down. But I want to speak to you in the middle of your pit. I want to ask you to make yourself available to God in whatever form or fashion He chooses—even if that means as a slave to Ishmaelite traders. Because if you do, you will one day discover His divine providence in using the pain to strengthen your spirit and to deliver you from here to that perfect place that is waiting for you.

God has a plan for you. Try not to fight the detours that are designed to take you to its culmination. Praise Him in the pain, even if it is just a faint word that falls off your parched lips. He knows what He is doing. He has great things up ahead for you.

CHAPTER THREE

The Pattern of Detours

 Not long ago I came upon a wreck on a road that leads from our national office to our local church. It appeared that the wreck had happened only minutes before I arrived. A car was completely overturned in the middle of a lane, and another one had skidded off to the side. An ambulance had arrived, and police cars, lights blazing, circled the disaster zone.

I and the other cars barely moved at all. We came to a halt and then crawled, at best. We scooted instead of driving. When a police officer would wave his hand up ahead, it seemed like he gave us only inches to move at a time. I sat there for what felt like forever, only eventually making it past the accident and through the line of cars.

I had left someone else at the office earlier who had also planned to make the trip over for another meeting. He had been tied up at the time and said he would arrive a little late. However when I finally did get to the church, he had pulled into the parking lot ahead of me. I asked him how he got there so soon. Didn't he come upon the same wreck that I had?

Actually, he had. But seeing the cars stalled ahead, he had taken his own detour and, as a result, beat me to the church.

He left later and arrived earlier, all because he chose a detour.

Sometimes we gain the wisdom to choose our own detours, but most of the time we are too caught up in just trying to make it—to push through—that we fail to recognize how a detour can actually take us further, faster. God knows the wisdom of detours, and so He uses them frequently on our behalf, forcing us down a path that is ultimately wiser—although at the time it may not appear that way.

God rarely takes us directly from where we are to where He wants us to go. More often than not, He disrupts the normal flow and directs us down a beaten path made up of unexpected curves, clefts, and challenges. And He most often does this without our consent.

That's what happened to Joseph, the seventeen-year-old teenager who found his life turned upside down by sudden, adverse circumstances. We left him in the last chapter in a pit. He's in a hole he can't get out of—a situation he can't resolve while facing a problem he cannot fix. In fact, this pit doesn't even have any water.

Not only can he not get out, but he doesn't have the nourishment to keep him going while in it. He's in what we would call a desperate situation, created by a toxic combination of his own family and his own immaturity. Here we have a royal kid about to be yanked from a royal mess in order to be made a slave, ultimately underneath a royal ruler.

That's a detour of epic proportions.

Most detours, though, have twists and turns. You have to go up here and then come back down here after which you head over there in order to finally make it to the main road again. Detours take you out of the way. If they don't, they aren't a detour.

One thing you can always expect on a detour is the unexpected.

But there are a few things, which I call *patterns*, that you can almost always count on showing up as well. There are a couple of predictable scenarios in detours. The first of which is that detours nearly always include a test.

Detours and Testing

Let me begin by defining what I mean by *test*. A test, or trial, in the biblical context, can be defined as:

An adverse circumstance either created or allowed by God in order to reveal to us the pathway of development in preparation for His purpose.

Second Chronicles 32:31 tells us that one reason God will use a test in our lives is to first reveal what is in our hearts. We read, "When the ambassadors of Babylon's rulers were sent to him to inquire about the miraculous sign that happened in the land, God left him to test him and discover what was in his heart." Trials call your faith to the witness stand to testify to the condition of your spiritual health.

Trials call your faith to the witness stand to testify to the condition of your spiritual health.

God already knows what is in your heart. But oftentimes, you and I don't. We can talk a good game, throw down spiritual platitudes, and even believe our own lies about ourselves sometimes. But the truth is the truth, and a test will always bring the truth to the surface. God knows that our hearts are deceitful and beyond cure (Jer. 17:9). Our hearts trick us, try us, and tempt us either to rely on ourselves too much or to even think too highly of who we are. In a test, God wants us to really see what is deep down inside of you and me. He wants us to know our capacity, both our potential and our limitations. Only when we know the truth can we address it, learn from it, and grow.

Every year I go the doctor for an annual physical exam. One part of the visit includes what is called a stress test. This is when the doctor puts me on a treadmill, after a nurse has attached all of these wires and devices to my chest, and asks me to walk. While walking he will increase the speed and the incline. This is because he wants to analyze the condition of my heart under various stressful situations.

I can tell my doctor all day long that I feel fine and that my heart is fine. But he's not going to take my word for it. Even if I believe what I'm saying is true. The doctor only knows if my heart is healthy by looking at how my heart responds to a test. As I huff and puff and sweat and complain on that treadmill, the doctor gets a good glimpse at the condition of my heart. He doesn't take my word for it. He looks at the paper and lets the data reveal the truth.

You and I can read our Bibles, go to church, participate in edifying conversations, and all the while feel that our spiritual hearts are fine. We can wave our hands in the air. Sing praises like everything is great. And we may even believe it ourselves. But God knows the true state of our heart, and He will often allow a test to reveal an accurate diagnosis. Not necessarily for His benefit, though, but for ours. He wants us to know the truth about ourselves—the good, the bad, and the ugly—because growth can only occur in a spirit of honesty.

God will often allow adverse circumstances, even painful circumstances, in our lives as a test in order to reveal, strengthen, and develop our hearts for His destiny. When you are going through a test, never mistake the hand of God for the hand of man.

Sure, as Joseph walked chained to the camels across the barren desert under the unforgiving sun, he could have blamed his brothers or even God. And we don't really know what he felt at that time. It's not recorded for us. So maybe he did.

But as Joseph matured through his detour over time, he eventually saw the hand of God guiding and directing it all. He didn't say that the Ishmaelite slave traders took him to Egypt years later when he reflected on where he was. He said God brought him to that place.

Because God really did bring him to that place.

Sometimes detours develop us. But sometimes they reroute us to an entire new location we wouldn't have even thought of going ourselves. It would be nice if God simply spoke to us like He did to Abraham and tell us to go to a land unknown, and we had the heart of Abraham and did it. But far too often we either fail to hear, or if we do hear, we fail to follow because it just doesn't make sense. So God ties us up behind some camels, and He gets us there anyhow. He's clever that way.

If you only see the camels, if you only see the ropes, if you only feel the hot sun or the hunger and emptiness night after night, and you miss seeing what God is doing, you will miss the divine purpose of the detour. God allows people to move us, shape us, and take us to our next step on the path He wants us to travel. So never think that just because it's people you see that it isn't God directing behind the scenes. God will often use people—even people in your family (even messed-up people in your family)—to move you to your destiny through a detour.

Joseph had many reasons to believe that God had abandoned him. Those feelings aren't wrong. You shouldn't feel guilt for responding to a pit with a question mark. Even the prophets were bold enough to question God. The prophet Jeremiah blamed God harshly when he wrote, "You deceived me, LORD, and I was deceived. You seized me and prevailed. I am a laughingstock all the time; everyone ridicules me" (Jer. 20:7). Even Christ asked why God had abandoned Him on the cross.

In your detours, remember that God is divine, but you are not. Emotions will go up and down, doubt is a natural response to life's trials, and God is a big God, He can take our words. But also remember as you face these feelings in the darkness of the deepest pit that God uses tests and trials—even detours—for our ultimate good. Ask Him in those times to help your unbelief and to give you trust. Ask Him to open your eyes to see spiritually beyond the physical. Ask Him to show you what He is trying to improve. Like a hot iron on a wrinkled shirt, the heat produces something good.

Joseph had some wrinkles.

He bragged on himself.

Tattled on his brothers.

He was immature.

But the heat of the scorching sun on the long walk from his home to Egypt no doubt began a process of smoothing his pride with the grace of humility and transforming his conceit into a confidence in God instead. God will place the hot iron of His molding grace on the wrinkles of our souls when He needs to. He does this because we have been created in His image and He desires that we reflect Him well. He will allow the fire of testing to bring steam to our hearts.

He's not being mean, though you might feel like He's being mean. I'm sure Joseph might have felt like He was being mean. God just wants the wrinkles ironed out so that He looks good when He identifies with you or me publicly in His name.

There is a true story that is told of a loggerhead turtle. A loggerhead turtle is a huge turtle, one of those mammoth ones you might see in a zoo. In this story, the female was getting ready to give birth, so she climbed up onto the sand dune in order to lay her turtle eggs. But after she did, she became disoriented and was not walking back to the water for some reason. That would have been the natural thing for her to do. But instead, she began walking further out on the sand.

Seeing this, some of the rangers came, and they put shackles on the loggerhead turtle because she was too big for them to lift. They tied up her legs and flipped her on her back. Then they attached a chain to the shackles and began to drag her upside down with a four-wheeler back to the water.

Now, this turtle's life has been jerked around, messed with, and she's no doubt in some discomfort, despite the best attempts by the rangers to be gentle with her. But in order for her life to be saved and her destiny preserved, that was the only viable option. If the rangers stood and shouted at this turtle to turn around, she wouldn't have understood. They could not have lured her toward the water with compelling hand motions. So they did what they had to do to get her where she needed to go.

Yes, God's Spirit does speak to us, and He can guide us with His Word. But more often than not, we, as the psalmist prayed, need to be led like the turtle—pulled, pushed, prodded. We read, "Do not be like a horse or mule, without understanding, that must be controlled with bit and bridle or else it will not come near you" (Ps. 32:9).

God cares too deeply for us to let us keep going down the wrong path or in the wrong direction. And He will drop an unexpected journey—a detour—in our way to get us turned around. Sometimes that may mean being flipped on our back or shackled on our feet. Sometimes that may mean being disoriented even within our own disorientation. Sometimes that might mean being dragged along until we finally feel the familiarity of our home. Once the turtle felt the water, she could be untied and put right side up again. Once she realized where she was, she was set free.

But in order for her to get to her destiny, she had to be flipped, turned, and dragged—just like Joseph from the pit to the camel-pull. God enters our situations in detours, and at times that requires a jerk, flip, tweaks, and pulls. We may yell in our hearts, "What are You doing to me, God? Where are You taking me? Why can't I understand?"

God answers, often too quietly for us to hear over our own shouts, "I'm taking you exactly where you need to be. Trust Me."

Friend, I don't know what pit you are in, or what path you are on. I don't know who did what to get you there or how long it's been. But I do know a promise from Someone who never lies. God will work it out for your good when you align your heart under His purpose and calling (Rom. 8:28).

Trust Him.

He has a destination up ahead for you.

And when you get there, you'll know you are home.

CHAPTER FOUR

The Purifying of Detours

 God has established patterns that pop up in people's lives when it comes to detours. These patterns often exist because a goal is being sought. Detours frequently provide the ground for development. There would be nothing worse than arriving at your destiny unprepared to fully carry it out. It's like the people who win the lottery only to lose their millions within a few years because they were unprepared for the responsibilities that come with that much money.

Another aspect I want us to look at with regard to patterns of detours is *training*. We are told in Scripture to learn from being tested so essentially testing, trials, and detours are places where we are trained. Like an athlete in the gym preparing for the field, this is the place where muscle strength and reflexes are sharpened.

Otherwise, the athlete gets to the field and cannot perform up to the level required to win.

First of all, there is a phrase we see pop up a lot with regard to Joseph's life. That phrase is, "And the LORD was with Joseph."

Over and over we see these words. Whether Joseph was in the pit, the prison, or the palace—the Lord was with him. Not only that, but we also see God's hand of favor with him causing whatever he touched to prosper and causing people to put things under his authority.

One thing to learn from God being with Joseph is that *Joseph was also with God*. In other words, Joseph did not allow the circumstances to compromise his spiritual relationship. Yes, it is easy to get mad at God when you face a trial or trouble in your life. But these are the times when you are to chase after God like you've never done before. These are the times when you are to draw near to Him.

When you fill a sponge full of water and then you add pressure to the sponge, water is going to flow out because it is full of water. When you are going through a trial and you feel the pressure of life caving in around you, how much of God comes out?

Or is it cussing, fussing, complaining, and blaming that comes out instead? Why are those things coming out? Because that is what you are full of.

A sponge only lets out what is in it. God was able to give Joseph favor because God was *in* Joseph during his trials.

This is important to know because God will do the same with and for you if you let Him. But so few people do. Most people fill themselves with entertainment, alcohol, gossip, distractions, bitterness, and things of that nature when life is not fair. But in order to have your detour take you to your destiny, you have to draw near to God. God will be near to, and *in*, you.

Joseph had cultivated a spiritual relationship along the way of his detours, as his priority became God. The key to making it during your season of testing is not found in your contacts, notoriety, name, or bank account. The key is found in your intimacy with the Lord. The Lord was with Joseph—and caused all that he did, no matter where he was, to prosper. There must be a spiritual relationship that drives you, particularly when life has gone left.

One of the purposes of a detour is to develop the capacity, skills, and character necessary to carry out your destiny. While Joseph was a slave in Potiphar's home, the Lord prospered him so that he became second-in-command in Potiphar's home. Little did he know that one day he would become second-in-command in the entire nation of Egypt. But God was preparing Joseph with the skills necessary to both follow and lead simultaneously. Joseph doesn't yet have the details of his destiny, but his obedience as a slave gave him the opportunity to learn skills he would use later on as a ruler.

Joseph acquired experience in leadership, management, problem-solving, and more. One of the problems we have today in our culture is that people want what they want right now. But if you can't handle where you are now, how will you handle more responsibility later? Scripture asks us in Jeremiah 12:5, "If you have raced with runners and they have worn you out, how can you compete with horses? If you stumble in a peaceful land, what will you do in the thickets of the Jordan?"

I always get a kick out of young pastors who ask me how they can get where I am now in ministry. Sometimes they have just graduated from seminary or Bible college, and they schedule a meeting with me to see if I can give them advice so that they might also gain a megachurch of our size or impact. I usually lean back in my chair, smile, and then say something similar to, "Go preach in a prison."

Without exception a look of, "You are kidding me, right?" comes over their faces. But it's the truth. It's the best advice I can give them. I didn't start out with a ten-thousand-member church or my messages being broadcast in two hundred countries and all over the United States. I started out on top of the bed of a pickup truck with no microphone, simply yelling as loud as I could to whoever was around. I started out on the corner where buses would come to pick up passengers, preaching the gospel of Jesus Christ (the only sermon I knew at the time). I started out in prison chapels. I preached in family rooms. I managed a staff of mostly family members and a congregation of the same when I first started out.

Training for greater things always takes place in lesser things. Be faithful, responsible, and content where you are now. That is one of the major secrets to God taking you further and giving you more.

God will not give you your destiny until you are ready to handle your destiny well. How can you take care of your destiny there if you are not yet taking care of the destiny He has you in right here? You have to get enough experience first with the "this" you are in now before He gives you the "that" you are hoping for.

Training for greater things always takes place in lesser things.

As a pastor, I am privy to a lot of complaints. One that I frequently hear is how hard it is as a Christian to work well in a non-Christian (secular) environment. Maybe the boss is not Christian, or the atmosphere is not Christian, but as we see from the life of Joseph—God was with Joseph where Joseph was. Joseph worked in a non-Christian environment. Potiphar was a pagan; he was not a believer. Joseph worked for a non-Christian company. But God blessed the Egyptian's house on account of Joseph.

As a believer, you should be the best employee, the most on-time employee, the most productive employee because the Lord is with you. Your relationship with God should bring favor to those around you due to *your* integrity, honesty, morality—not theirs. You should stand out as Joseph stood out—wherever you are. Let those around you see Jesus in you, not just hear you talk about your morals and your beliefs.

The best witness often comes from behavior, not words. In Genesis 39:3–4 we read, "When his master saw that the LORD was with him and that the LORD made everything he did successful, Joseph found favor in his master's sight and became his personal attendant. Potiphar also put him in charge of his household and placed all that he owned under his authority."

The Bible doesn't say that the master heard Joseph running his mouth all day long talking about his God while getting nothing done. Joseph didn't turn in sloppy work, complaining that he didn't really agree with the values set forth by the company anyhow. No, the master saw that the Lord was with Joseph and that the Lord caused all Joseph did to prosper. In business, that's the bottom line. Move the bottom line up and you get the attention of those in charge. It's difficult to argue with the bottom line. It's difficult to not be promoted when it is evident that God is with you and prospering all you do. This also means Joseph was not silent about his faith. He had made it clear to Potiphar that his attitudes, actions, and work ethic were tied directly to his relationship with God.

When I was only a teenager, I went to work as a dishwasher in a catering service. My job was to wash dishes. It wasn't that difficult. I was to wash the dirty dishes that came into the kitchen—and wash them by hand. The owner of the catering service was a business-minded Jewish man who juggled multiple balls in the air and wore multiple hats. From time to time, he would come into the area where I worked to check on things. I always greeted him warmly and asked if he had anything more for me to do, seeing as I stayed on top of my job and always finished it early.

Over time, he took notice of my work and eventually asked me to become his personal driver, as well as the driver for his kids to all of their weekend activities. He promoted me.

Over the next few years of taking good care of his kids, we developed a relationship. He saw potential in me and pulled me aside one day to offer to pay my way to go to college for the first year. He wanted to invest in my personal development and thought this was the best way to do that.

We didn't share the same religion. I went away to a Christian college. But God used this man to promote me in my life to a position where I would later be used by Him to minister to so many people, in so many ways.

Friend, always—always—always be faithful where you are. Be diligent, even if you are just washing dishes. Or just driving a car full of some kids to a sporting event. You never know what God is going to use in someone else's mind and heart to move you further ahead into your destiny.

Joseph's job at Potiphar's house was not his ultimate destiny. It was a stepping-stone to his ultimate destiny. It was his preparation point to promotion. But since he approached it as if it were his destiny—he worked hard, received favor, managed well—the Lord used it for His purpose. Far too often, we are chasing our destiny so much that we forget to maximize the location where we are right now.

God does not live in time or space. To God, today is in the same time zone as ten years ago. It's also in the same time zone as ten years ahead. To God, our destiny plays out simultaneously wherever we are. Whether we are in a preparation stage of destiny, a connection and networking stage of destiny, or simply a waiting stage of destiny—God's purpose for our lives is always a current purpose. It's a *right now* destiny.

Yet, too many believers lose both contentment and gratitude for the place they are *right now* because they are always waiting for something greater. They are always looking ahead to achieve their destiny. Rather than realizing, as a child of God, your destiny is in you now, simply unfurling into its complete manifestation someday. Honor each moment, each job, each person with the knowledge that destiny lives in you now, perhaps in seed form—but each step, each day, each moment, each lesson, and each interaction play a part in the road map of your life.

When you are driving, you don't simply arrive at your destination. If you were to look disdainfully on the road you take—thinking only of the destination—you may never get there. If you refuse to drive on the two-lane country road, you will never reach your final location. Destiny is a mind-set that allows you to embrace and maximize the power of where you are right now as you look forward to a greater release of your purpose, influence, and impact in the future.

When you learn how to focus on your relationship with God in any and every situation you are in, you put less pressure on the situation—whether that's a job, relationship, hobby, etc.—to be everything for you. Joseph was just a slave in a house, but God was with him and gave him favor. Be careful not to complain about where you are because when you honor God and your relationship with God in it, He has a way of giving you favor in situations you never even imagined.

God cares more for the development of the dreamer than the actual dream itself. He cares more for your personal growth than your final destination. Because if you are not developed or matured, you will ultimately mess up the dream and final destination when you get there. Most of us have dreams. But God wants to make sure you have the strength in your shoulders to bear the weight of that dream once you get there. He doesn't want you to collapse underneath a pile of purpose. Detours are designed to develop that. They are designed to strengthen muscles of contentment, gratitude, faith, love, humility, and obedience.

Temptation

Another pattern on detours that people often run into is the pattern of temptation. Joseph faced a test. He faced training. But he also faced temptation—*a solicitation to do evil and disobey God*.

Keep in mind, temptation itself is not sin. Being tempted is not the same as sinning. Sinning is *when you yield to the temptation*. Satan uses temptation to move us away from the will of God. He offers the down payment of pleasure, numbing pain, or distraction so that he can come back later for full payment with interest.

The Lord sent Joseph to Potiphar's house on a detour. He also knew that Mrs. Potiphar was going to be there as well. We are told in the passage that Joseph was a modern-day superstar in looks and build. He was handsome in both form and appearance. He had six-pack abs. He was a beast, eye candy for the ladies. After enough eye candy, Mrs. Potiphar decided she wanted more than just something to look at. So she made an advance at Joseph, inviting him to become intimate with her.

But Joseph refused to have relations with Mrs. Potiphar out of honor and respect for his master, Mr. Potiphar. He also refused out of honor and obedience to God. We read, "No one in this house is greater than I am. He has withheld nothing from me except you, because you are his wife. So how could I do such a great evil and sin against God?" (Gen. 39:9). Joseph saw sin as a relational issue. He realized he had a master on the earth as well as one in heaven, causing him to run even though it meant leaving valuables behind.

Mrs. Potiphar didn't take no for an answer. Scripture tells us that day after day she continued to flirt, continued to make her proposition, continued to put pressure on him to give in to what she wanted. Eventually his rejection left her annoyed, irritated, and humiliated to the point that she accused him of the very thing he did not do. She accused him of rape. They say that hell hath no fury like a woman scorned.

Joseph had not given in because of his love for God. He valued his relationship with God more than he valued momentary pleasure. It wasn't easy, I'm sure. But it was the right decision. Joseph demonstrated he could be trusted under pressure. A right decision that subsequently landed him in another pit—this time a prison. Have you ever made a right decision only to later feel you are being punished for doing just that? Little did Joseph know that he needed to be in the prison in order to one day wind up standing before Pharaoh in a time of need. It must have seemed confusing and contradictory to obey God and have God seemingly punish you by tossing you in prison. But that's what detours do—they sometimes confuse us. They sometimes cause us to question and to doubt. They sometimes look irrational and illogical.

This is because we cannot see where the detour is taking us. We can only see the pit and the problems.

Detours involve negative experiences that God either creates or allows. Never mistake the hand of God for the hand of man or for the hand of Satan. While Satan uses temptations to derail us from our destiny, God uses those same temptations to detour us to our destiny. Our responsibility is not to yield. Joseph could have easily believed that Mrs. Potiphar landed him in jail. But God simply used her to put him in the place He needed him to be. That's why forgiveness is such a critical part of reaching the full manifestation of your destiny. Because if you harbor bitterness toward those God used to move you further along in life—through negative realities—you are not seeing fully. You are not seeing how God used them to push you ahead to a place you probably would have never gone on your own.

I can guarantee you that Joseph would have never decided to request a transfer to prison. He would have never gone to Mr. Potiphar, thanked him for the job, and asked to be moved to a prison instead.

But that is where God needed him to be in order to be in position for his greater destiny and kingdom purpose.

Many times, negative realities in our lives have a way of pushing us into situations and locations we would never have gone had we not been nudged. So be careful if you harbor bitterness to those who have hurt you. Consider how God may be using them to develop you, move you, and position you for your greatest promotion yet. God loves you enough to develop you for where He is taking you. Say "no" to that which breaks His heart—temptation. But realize that you saying "no" may not immediately bring you reward. You will need to be patient for that to come.

Let go of any grudge you have toward someone who has offended you, accused you, or moved you into a place you did not want to go. And let God show you why it happened and what He is doing through it. When you do, you will discover the purifying grace of acceptance and the power of peace in living out your destiny both now and in the future.

CHAPTER FIVE

The Proof of Detours

 Part of my role as pastor involves mentoring and counseling. With a fairly large church, you can imagine the number of calls I get. I'm grateful to have the opportunity to guide members through various situations in life. I can honestly say I enjoy this aspect of being a pastor immensely.

Not too long ago one of the men from the church came over to my home to meet with me. He had been going through a rough time. As he sat in my family room, head hung low, he lifted his eyes to mine and said, "Pastor, I feel as if my detour has met another detour, and they got married and had a baby." In other words, he felt as if he were running into detour after detour after detour and that the detours merely kept replicating and multiplying rather than taking him anywhere meaningful.

It is easy to feel that way when God is taking you to your destiny. As I mentioned before, God rarely ever moves you from where you are to where He wants you to be without taking you on a road trip first. He doesn't go from A to B to C. He goes from A to Z to T to R to F to D, meandering you to your destiny. Before you can ever get to where God wants you to be, He has to do some twists and turns. This is because in life, as it is often on the road, detours exist because construction is taking place. When you are on a highway and there is a detour, it is usually because workers are trying to fix, build, correct, or improve something.

Similarly, God will take us on a detour because He is constructing something in our lives as well. Granted, detours are anything but convenient. They take you out of the way. They are longer than you originally had planned to travel. But they are necessary. God is more interested in your development than your arrival. He cares more for your character than your comfort, your purity than your productivity.

In this chapter and the next, I want us to look at ways you can use to help you determine and confirm that you truly are on a detour rather than simply experiencing a spot of bad luck.

How can you know that this is a God-ordained detour rather than things just aren't working out for you right now?

How can you discern that you are not under the circumstances of normal life and consequences but rather in a situation that God Himself has guided you into?

There are several ways you can know this. I want to start with the reason for the suffering you may be experiencing. If and when you are suffering for doing good rather than doing bad—we also call that being persecuted for righteousness—you can know that you are in God's plan of a detour.

After Joseph had worked in his master Potiphar's home for some time, he had earned Potiphar's trust. So much so that Joseph was over pretty much everything in his home. Yet, despite performing such great and reliable work for Potiphar, he eventually wound up in jail.

Potiphar's wife had noticed that Joseph was attractive, so she made advances at him—day after day (Gen. 39:6–10). However, Joseph was wise enough to pass on the pass. He was wise enough from God's perspective, that is.

From man's perspective that decision to refuse the request of his master's wife landed him on the hot seat and ultimately in another pit as she, in her pain of rejection, accused him of rape. We read, "When his master heard the story his wife told him—'These are the things your slave did to me'—he was furious and had him thrown into prison, where the king's prisoners were confined. So Joseph was there in prison" (Gen. 39:19–20).

When you find yourself, like Joseph, struggling or suffering out of a decision you made in obedience to God, *your struggle is right where God wants you to be.*

If we look more closely at the biblical account of Joseph and Potiphar's wife, it clearly tells us that Joseph refused her out of obedience to the Lord.

> "Look," he said to his master's wife, "with me here my master does not concern himself with anything in his house, and he has put all that he owns under my authority. No one in this house is greater than I am. He has withheld nothing from me except you, because you are his wife. So how could I do such a great evil and sin against God?" (Gen. 39:8–9)

Joseph recognized the blessings in his life and felt gratitude for how far God had taken him—from a pit left to die, to a position of great authority and responsibility. Knowing his source was God Himself, Joseph made his decision on God alone. "How could I do such a great evil and sin against God?" he told her. We are never told this, but it could be that Potiphar's wife was a temptation to him. It could be that she was attractive—the servants were away, Potiphar, also, was gone—and Joseph may have felt something for her. We don't know.

What I do know is that a sacrifice isn't a sacrifice unless it costs you something. And a temptation isn't a temptation unless it's tempting. Joseph turned her offer down out of his conviction before God, not necessarily out of a lack of interest. That's important to keep in mind as you go through life and make decisions. As God did by testing Abraham, by asking him to offer up the child of his heart as a sacrifice (Genesis 22), He will often ask us to sacrifice, or overcome a temptation, out of our love and obedience for Him that costs us something. It cost Joseph the loss of his clothes, his job, and his freedom.

Sometimes the obedience itself is the persecution and the pain. But other times, God takes it a step further—as He did with Joseph—and a detour comes into play. Joseph wound up in jail because he chose his love for God over his own pleasures. He experienced what we read in 2 Timothy 3:12, "In fact, all those who want to live a godly life in Christ Jesus will be persecuted." Peter says we are to suffer for righteousness, not unrighteousness (1 Pet. 2:20).

If you are a serious believer and you are making decisions based on what God wants over what you or even your friends or the society in general wants, the Bible says you can bet your bottom dollar there will be persecution. There will be suffering. There will be sacrifice. It may come in different shapes, sizes, and forms, but it will come. Negative repercussions follow those who live by faith.

In fact, if you never experience negative repercussions in your life because of godly decisions, then that could be an indication that you are not living solidly as a Christian. The Bible says clearly that those who make their choices based on their faith (who desire to live godly) will be persecuted. Everyone is not going to be your friend if you are serious about Jesus. This is because you will have to make choices that go against the grain. When you march to a different drumbeat, you walk out of step with the cadence of this world order.

I got a phone call not too long ago from a brokenhearted woman I had been counseling. Through tears, she told me that her boyfriend had broken up with her because she wouldn't sleep with him. She had thought he was the love of her life and had believed they would be together forever, but when she wouldn't give in to his advances, he went elsewhere.

I've gotten calls from other people who have literally been fired from jobs because they refused to compromise on a deal or go along with a program that was not morally upright. They made a decision for righteousness, and there was a price tag that had to be paid.

So let me tell you up front—I would love for you to visit my church, or listen to me on the radio, or pick up a book I've penned, and have it be full of me sharing how to come get your blessings in life. I would love to be able to tell you that nothing will ever go wrong in your life, especially if you follow after God with all your heart. But I'd be lying. I'd be telling a fib. I'd be spinning a tale because Scripture says the exact opposite. The "name it and claim it" we find in God's Word looks very different from the one purported in pulpits all over our land. If you name a godly life in Christ Jesus, you can be sure to claim persecutions. That's what the Bible says. And that's what you can count on.

Daniel got thrown into the lions' den because he wouldn't compromise on the job.

Paul was thrown in prison.

Joseph was left in a pit.

Stephen was stoned.

Meshach, Shadrach, and Abednego got tossed into a fiery furnace for refusing to bow to an idol. They suffered the effects of their decision not to compromise their faith. It is unfortunate today how few Christians are willing to bear consequences for their commitment. Too many believers today are moving along as cultural Christians or convenient Christians; not so many are seriously committed Christians.

The most critical test you will ever face is the test for suffering when you did nothing wrong. When you do exactly what God has told you to do and you have to pay a price tag for it, you are paying a penalty for righteousness' sake. You are on an intended detour that will test and strengthen both your character and your resolve if you will let it.

> *The most critical test you will ever face is the test for suffering when you did nothing wrong.*

Joseph winds up in jail due to his choice to honor God. He is suffering for his faith while being right smack-dab in the middle of the will of God. He wasn't in a pleasant place. He was in a dungeon. The king had his own private prison for people like Joseph. We read in the book of Psalms that Joseph was tested there by the Lord. He was bound in shackles and chains. It says, "He called down famine against the land and destroyed the entire food supply. He had sent a man ahead of them—Joseph, who was sold as a slave. They hurt his feet with shackles; his neck was put in an iron collar. Until the time his prediction came true, the word of the Lord tested him" (Ps. 105:16–19).

Not only was Joseph in a dark place; he was in a deep, dark pit with limited mobility as well. He was shackled and collared, unable to move himself. Trapped—in the middle of God's will.

A lot of people think that when things go bad, they are out of God's will. But if you were to do a careful study of the Bible, things often go bad *in* God's will. It is on these detours that the Lord does to us what He did to Joseph. He tests us as He "tested him." See, it's easy to give God praise and our allegiance when things are going well. But when you are bound, shackled, removed from sunlight— removed from all hope—that reveals the true constitution of your heart. Do you throw in the towel and give up? Or do you press on in obedience to the Lord, even though you can't understand the meaning of the detour you are on?

Do you remember in school when the teacher graded on the curve? At first, when this decision was announced, it gave everyone hope. It made us believe we had a chance at a great grade because if the subject matter was difficult, our doing poorly may be good enough after all. But then, if your class was anything like mine, there would always be that one person, or two, who would some- how manage to ace the test even though the rest of us got low Bs or even Cs. This person would put up an amazing score and cause the curve not to mean much of anything at all. We called that "break- ing the curve" where I came from.

When you are chosen by God to represent Him in the culture, He wants you to break the curve. He wants you to set the standard so high that you truly reflect Him in your life. When you choose righteousness, and suffer because of it, the Lord will often allow continual trials because He knows they will test you even further. They will produce in you the qualities and character that will make you more like Jesus Christ. Joseph had a glorious destiny ahead of him. He had a destiny that would save people—save nations—from literal starvation. But Joseph wasn't going to arrive at his destiny until his character was molded and shaped in a manner where he could handle it well.

The greater the calling, the deeper the pit.

The higher the destiny, the tighter the shackles.

The more glorious the future, the more persecuted the present.

Learn to view suffering (when suffering for good) through the lens of the Lord. He has a purpose for the pain if you will discover how to hang in there—like Joseph—even when life does not seem fair.

CHAPTER SIX

The Presence of Detours

 In the last chapter we looked at one way to discover if you are on a God-inspired detour or simply going through the consequences of bad choices. We saw how suffering for doing what is right is often a way God tests us. Joseph wound up in jail because he refused to dishonor God by accepting the advances of Potiphar's wife.

Another way you can discern you are on a detour designed by God is that in the midst of your suffering for doing good, God shows you His presence. He shows you His favor. God joins you in the pit.

God didn't keep Daniel from the lions' den; He met him in it.

He didn't keep Shadrach, Meshach, and Abednego from the fiery furnace; He joined them in it.

He didn't keep Joseph from being a slave to Potiphar; He gave him favor in it—to the point that Joseph wound up with authority over Potiphar's home and all his possessions. Later, when Joseph was tossed onto another detour into prison, God went to the prison with him as well. It says in Genesis 39:21, "But the LORD was with Joseph and extended kindness to him. He granted him favor in the eyes of the prison warden."

The second proof for knowing you are where God wants you to be in your detour is that God doesn't deliver you from it but rather joins you in it. I know you may be praying, like Joseph may have himself, "Lord, get me out of this jail. Get me out of this detour!" But it may not be the right time to get you out. So if God is not ready to deliver you from it, look for Him in it.

Do you see His hand of favor on you? Do you see Him giving you favor to others around you? Can you experience His presence with you? Are you open to looking for it?

Look for Him to give you light in the midst of the darkness.

I recently spent some time with a large group of singles when they had an evening of fellowship on our church campus. I shared with them what Joseph's secret was in being a successful single the years that he was. This secret is recorded for us in the book of Acts. We read, "The patriarchs became jealous of Joseph and sold him into Egypt, but God was with him" (Acts 7:9). Joseph's success was that God was with him. He was with him in the pit, in Potiphar's house, and even in the prison.

The key to victory in whatever situation you are facing is not first where you are or what you are going through but rather who is with you while you're there. In prison, "the LORD was with Joseph and extended kindness to him." We see how God's presence and kindness showed up in the next few verses, "The warden put all the prisoners who were in the prison under Joseph's authority, and he was responsible for everything that was done there. The warden did not bother with anything under Joseph's authority, because the LORD was with him, and the LORD made everything that he did successful" (Gen. 39:22–23).

Joseph got a promotion in jail. God didn't change the situation—Joseph was still in jail. But in the detour God promoted him.

The way God shows up isn't always by delivering you from something—sometimes it is delivering you in it. If God is granting you favor in the midst of a trial, test, or detour, that may be a hint that He isn't ready to deliver you from that detour just yet. You may be wondering how to tell if it really is God and not just circumstances. Let's look at a pattern God often uses. If you'll remember when Joseph was a slave in Potiphar's house, Potiphar promoted him to make him head over everything. It says, "The LORD was with Joseph, and he became a successful man, serving in the household of his Egyptian master. When his master saw that the LORD was with him and that the LORD made everything he did successful, Joseph found favor in his master's sight and became his personal attendant. Potiphar also put him in charge of his household and placed all that he owned under his authority" (vv. 2–4).

Later when Joseph languished in jail, the same thing happened. The jailer took notice of him and, again, put him in charge. God showed up, not once, but twice in a similar way. Scripture often says that by "two or three witnesses" a matter will be confirmed.

When the Lord shows up twice in your life in a similar fashion, pay attention! He is talking. It's not bad luck. It's not good luck. It's not chance. It is God confirming He is doing this on purpose because He is giving you a double witness.

When Gideon needed proof that he was really hearing from God, he put the animal skin out and asked for God to make it dry on one side and wet on the other. The next day he flipped it over and asked for the opposite. God will often reveal Himself in groups of two. Not always, but there is often a pattern you can see if you look through spiritual eyes. Look for how God might be speaking to you by doing or allowing something twice in your life. Ask Him for wisdom to discern His hand of favor and what it means. Sometimes it may mean no real change in your situation— you may still be in the pit. But just knowing you are not alone is enough to give you the strength to wait well.

Have you ever experienced a lot of turbulence on an airplane? I have. There have been occasions when the plane seems to be jumping all over the place. Grown men and women are screaming, buckling up their already tightened seatbelts. The looks on their faces show apparent nervousness.

But then you hear a voice come over the loudspeaker.

You recognize the voice of the captain. The captain explains that you are in a rough spot right now but that in another ten to fifteen minutes you will be out of it. Somehow just hearing that he knows what's going on relieves the stress. Hearing the captain's voice didn't stop the turbulence or the bumps. But hearing his voice calmed you as the plane continued to maneuver through it.

God doesn't always take us out of our detours, but knowing He is with us can produce calm amid the turbulence of life. When the financial, relational, health, employment, or whatever situation won't seem to get restored in your life, listen for God's voice. Do you recognize His presence? Can you feel His favor despite the adversities and pain around you?

God was with Joseph, in the pit and in the prison, because He had a plan.

Serving While Suffering

Another proof that you are on your way to your destiny when you are stuck on a detour is when God gives you a ministry to other people who are going through the same or similar things that you are. He gives you people to serve while you are suffering.

The next portion of Joseph's story reveals this to us in his life:

After this, the Egyptian king's cupbearer and baker offended their master, the king of Egypt. Pharaoh was angry with his two officers, the chief cupbearer and the chief baker, and put them in custody in the house of the captain of the guard in the prison where Joseph was confined. The captain of the guard assigned Joseph to them, and he became their personal attendant. And they were in custody for some time. (Gen. 40:1–4)

Two of Pharaoh's most trusted servants, his cupbearer and his baker, got in some hot water themselves. Since they were under the sentence of death, they were probably seen as part of an assassination plot to Pharaoh. Landing in jail, they came under Joseph's care. Later on in the story we will discover that these two jailbirds hold the key to Joseph's destiny. But before God would ever use that key to unlock anything in Joseph's life, he first wanted Joseph to help these two men. Joseph had to learn to look beyond his own misery and see how he could be used to help others before God would promote him to his ultimate kingdom assignment.

The tendency when you are suffering is to be self-absorbed. It's a normal tendency in all of us. If you hear about other people with problems, you don't care to help them because you want to spend all of your emotional energy on nursing your own wounds. But the key to overcoming your own suffering is actually the opposite. You are to look for people going through a similar thing as yourself and find a way to minister to them while you wait on God to minister to you. Joseph, noticing their sad faces, ministered to them (Gen. 40:6–8).

What many people do is get selfish in their suffering. But the righteous response to suffering is to help someone else. One of the ways God moves you through your detours is through your ministry. If you are unwilling to minister to someone else, you could be delaying your own destiny by increasing the length of your detour. Being self-centered may actually cause you to miss out on the blessing God has in store for you.

When the two men in jail needed someone to help them, Joseph was there. Joseph wasn't so busy wallowing in his own self-pity that he didn't have time for anyone else. The two men had a dream, and dreams were Joseph's specialty. Interpreting both dreams for the men, he used the gift God had given him to help someone

What many people do is get selfish in their suffering.

else. We'll see later on how Joseph's being willing to interpret their dreams actually got him out of the prison.

If you want to see God show up in your detour and take you to your destiny, look for other people to serve. You don't have to be sophisticated about it; just use the gift God has given you when you see someone who may need it. God wants to use your detours to help others in theirs as well. Noah ministered while he waited for rain. Ruth ministered while she waited for God to change her situation. Rebecca drew water for a stranger's camels while she waited for God to provide her with a mate. They all ministered in the midst of waiting—during the delay of their detour.

Be careful not to miss your ministry because of your misery. God uses ministry to recharge your spiritual batteries while you wait. As 2 Corinthians tells us, God has a reason for the comfort, favor, and kindness He gives us in the middle of our troubles. It says, "He comforts us in all our affliction, so that we may be able to comfort those who are in any kind of affliction, through the comfort we ourselves receive from God. For as the sufferings of Christ overflow to us, so through Christ our comfort also overflows" (1:4–5). God not only desires for us to connect vertically with Him. He also wants to use us to connect horizontally with each other. It needs to be both ways to fully live out the greatest and second greatest commandments, which are to love God first and love others as ourselves. If you are in a detour, find a way to encourage someone else who is in the same or similar situation that you are in. You rarely find someone alone on a detour. Typically, there is a line of cars being rerouted and moving slowly.

Stuck Too Long

Lastly, and probably the most discouraging of the four proofs that you are on a God-ordained detour, is when God postpones your release. He puts off your change. He pushes back your deliverance—which is exactly what happened to Joseph in jail.

After interpreting the two inmates' dreams, he asked the cup-bearer one thing. He asked him to remember him when he got out. Joseph said, "But when all goes well for you, remember that I was with you. Please show kindness to me by mentioning me to Pharaoh, and get me out of this prison. For I was kidnapped from the land of the Hebrews, and even here I have done nothing that they should put me in the dungeon" (Gen. 40:14–15).

Joseph simply asked to be remembered when the cupbearer got out. That's all. That's not a lot. No one would consider that asking too much of anyone. Joseph willingly interpreted his dream and gave him hope about his future. In return, all he asked for was a way out of his own prison situation. "Yet the chief cupbearer did not remember Joseph; he forgot him" (v. 23). The cupbearer went on his way, leaving Joseph in a seemingly unending delay.

Friend, you may not like what I am about to say, but I've seen it in Scripture, and I've seen it in people's lives enough times to believe that it is a pattern of God. You are exactly where you are supposed to be when it looks like God has you on the precipice of disaster. When it looks like He is just about to come through for you in the most hopeless of times. When it looks like relief must be creeping up over the horizon . . . but then it ducks back down and disappears.

When God goes left and you needed a right, that is often proof positive that you are right where He wants you to be.

This is similar to when Martha and Mary lost their brother Lazarus when he was sick and then died. They asked Jesus why He delayed in coming to them while he was still alive. Christ's answer to Martha and Mary is a similar answer to Joseph in jail and each of us when we face destiny's detours—God has a specific reason for His delays. It is in order to show His hand all the more powerful and to deepen our faith.

Do you feel stuck? Do you feel like you are in a situation that just won't end, despite all the prayers you have prayed and attempts at overcoming it yourself?

You feel like God has forgotten you even though you have tried to honor Him in your thoughts and actions. Then, He shows you little clues of His presence here or there. He uses you to minister to others in the midst of your pain. And just when it looks like He is about to deliver you—you've found the right person, the right job, your purpose, health or finances are about to turn around for good—you face yet another delay when it appears that God has slammed the door of opportunity and deliverance in your face. It is easiest to give up in times like those.

How must Joseph have felt when he saw his way out of a dungeon he didn't deserve, but then day after day passed and there came no word? There came no call from up above. There came no key to deliverance. That's enough to test any man's faith—when you feel forgotten, especially after serving so well.

But remember—a delay does not mean a denial.

A delay occurs when God is continuing to prepare your destiny for you and you for your destiny in order to fulfill His greater kingdom purposes. God had a glorious purpose for Joseph to fulfill, but it would require a few more years in jail. Yes, *years*.

God's timetable is rarely our own. His detours may last much longer than we want. But when you reach your destiny—as when Joseph finally reached his—you will look back with wonder and exclaim that God was right, and even kind, all along.

CHAPTER SEVEN

The Promotion of Detours

 While I was studying and preaching through this topic of detours recently, I got a reminder of what happens on a detour in life. My wife Lois and I were headed back from Denver, Colorado, following a speaking event earlier that morning. It was Saturday, and if you know me at all, you know I don't ever miss a Sunday. Getting back to Dallas was a necessity. And as we boarded the plane in sunny Colorado, I assumed our return home was a sure thing.

The plane took off on time, and we were on our way back to our destination. Just an hour and forty-five minutes away. Yet two-thirds into the flight, the pilot came on the speaker and let us know that storms were brewing in Dallas, and we would have to be rerouted to Oklahoma City.

Now, Oklahoma City was not in my plans. I had not requested it, desired it, anticipated it, or even thought about it. But somebody else was in control. And the somebody else who was in control told me I wasn't going where I thought I was headed after all. He proved to be right, and we landed in Oklahoma City.

Not only were we in Oklahoma City, but we were stuck on an airplane. They wouldn't pull up to a gate. They wouldn't let us off. We were stuck on the tarmac inside the plane indefinitely. The pilot kept saying it would be another fifteen minutes. Then later he would come on and say that it's going to be another twenty minutes. Two hours later, he came back on again and said it would be another fifteen minutes. Lois and I were stuck on that plane in Oklahoma City for hours!

Finally, after a delay that seemed to go on forever due to circumstances out of our control, the pilot came back on and said we were about to take off now to head to Dallas. Relief flooded my body and my mind. I would make it back in time to preach. Gratefully, I buckled up my seat belt, leaned back, and waited for the short flight to commence. The engines roared, we barreled down the runway, the plane began to take off.

And that is when it happened.

The plane began to slow down.

Again.

You heard me right. The plane slowed down, brakes went to work, and we stayed on the tarmac. The pilot's voice came on a little later, "I'm sorry," he said. "But new storms have shown up in the Dallas/Fort Worth area, and so we are not able to take off. It will be another fifteen minutes."

Fifteen minutes, right! It wasn't fifteen minutes. It wasn't even twenty minutes. Another hour later, the pilot came back on and said things had cleared up and we were ready to take off again. You can bet I didn't bother to buckle up my seat belt this time. But the unthinkable happened; the plane actually took off, and I finally was on my way back to my destiny—Dallas, Texas, and Oak Cliff Bible Fellowship.

Or so I thought.

When the plane landed in Dallas, the pilot came back on (you can imagine I was tired of hearing from this pilot by now). He said, "Ladies and gentlemen, I have some good news, and I have some bad news. The good news is that we have landed in Dallas. The bad news is that there are no gates available. It will be another forty-five minutes to an hour before we can anticipate pulling up to a gate."

Needless to say, I was past the point of evangelically-ticked-off. It would be more than an hour before we disembarked. Our short one hour and forty-five minute trip had turned into a seven-hour ordeal!

I had been on an extended detour.

Some of you reading this may feel like that's the story of your life. You planned to be over here by now, and yet you are in a holding pattern. You don't know when the plane called *destiny* is going to land. You may be growing frustrated or have even found yourself losing hope. The pilot says to "buckle up," and you don't even bother anymore. You've been stuck on the tarmac of trials and tribulation, and you may have even forgotten where you intended to go all along.

But I want to encourage you if this is how you feel today. I want to remind you that God has a purpose for the pain and a destination at the end of the detour. When your preparation meets God's purpose—your time connects with His time—you are ready to move from detour to destiny.

Always remember when looking at the detours in your life that God is crafting your destination while He is developing you. He is crafting a purpose while developing a person. When the person is prepared for the purpose and the purpose is prepared for the person, that is when God creates a hookup—and that hookup is called *destiny*.

The problem occurs when God has prepared the purpose but the person is not yet ready for it. When the preparation has not been allowed to do its work in order to produce focus, maturity, character, and faith, it only elongates the detour. Similar to the storms still brewing in Dallas that caused our delay from Denver, the storms in your soul—when left unchecked and unaddressed—create delays in you reaching your destiny.

A Lesson about Life

Joseph's detour started when he was seventeen years old. By the time we reach Genesis 41, he's thirty years old. That's thirteen long years of wandering and waiting, not really knowing why God had allowed so many twists and turns along the way. It was a long detour, no doubt.

But it had an exit.

It had a destination.

It had a purpose tied to the delays.

It had an end to its untimely beginning.

And from Joseph's example, we can pick up on some clues that can help us recognize when God is ready to bring us to the end of a detour. The first sign is when God disappoints you just when you thought He was coming through for you.

I know you didn't expect to read that. You probably expected to read something like, "When God gives you a glimpse of your destiny on the horizon and points you in the right direction," or something similar. But God doesn't work the way we want Him to sometimes. He works in His own mysterious ways because He knows what works best for each one of us.

He works in His own mysterious ways because He knows what works best for each one of us.

A lesson from the life of Joseph, in regards to detours, is that just when it looks like God is about to deliver you, and He disappoints you instead, you are on your path to your destiny.

In chapter 41 of Genesis, we read about this with Joseph. We looked at it in the last chapter. Joseph had interpreted the baker and the cupbearer's dreams, and then asked if the cupbearer would remember him when he got out of jail. I'm sure Joseph may have felt he was finally going to be delivered. He had found his way out. He was tired of the prison, the darkness, the dank and smelly surroundings. He helped out someone else so he expected some reciprocity for his good deed. Maybe he felt a little like I did when the airplane started down the runway to take off that first time out of Oklahoma City. I could imagine myself almost in the air and close to home. But then the captain put the brakes on, and we were stuck again. It would almost have been more merciful to have just sat on the tarmac longer than to have us almost take off only to abort it seconds before doing so.

It looked like, to Joseph, that God had finally brought someone into his life who could deliver him. It looked like his day had finally arrived.

But things went left before they ever went right. Things stalled before they ever took off. The cupbearer forgot Joseph. And Joseph had no way to get his attention again.

I was on the phone at midnight the other night talking with a brother who was bemoaning the circumstances in his life. I went over this principle with him, that when God disappoints you at just the time when it looked like He was going to deliver you, it's really a time when God is telling you, "Get ready for where I'm taking you." When my friend discovered that God often works that way, it didn't change his circumstances, but it did change the way he saw it. It changed his patience level in the midst of a challenging situation.

As bad as it may feel when God disappoints you, it is actually a great thing because He is setting you up for where He is taking you. He is getting you prepared—you are almost there. Just hang on a bit longer and don't throw in the towel just yet. He's strengthening your faith, gratitude, and resolve.

Among other things.

He's also preparing the place (or person) to which He is taking you—for you.

Keep that in mind too. Your destiny may not yet be ready for you. God may be preparing the place you are going (or the person He is going to connect you with) *for your sake,* as well.

So while a delay may feel bad and disappointing, it is wise for the captain to put his passengers through the detour. If the captain would have been impatient sitting in Oklahoma City and taken off instead of waiting out the storm, who knows what might have happened. If he would have tried to land the plane in the middle of strong winds and lightning, none of us might be here today. See, your detour isn't only about you. It is also about the other passengers in your life—God cares about them and their good too. It is often, also, about your destination being ready to receive you.

There is another reason why God will often delay your deliverance when it looks as if it is on the verge. This is because God wants to be sure He is given the credit for what happens.

If Joseph's contact in the jail would have sprung him after he became free himself, then Joseph might take the credit himself. And we all know what happened to Joseph when his ego got too large a few years earlier. So God allowed him to get right to the edge of deliverance—in his own strength—and then backed him back out. He did this so he would know that it wasn't through human effort that he reached his destiny. It wasn't because he did somebody a favor. It would only be because of God Himself. God didn't allow the cupbearer to remember Joseph. He does similar things in our own situations too.

Because when God wants to do His thing in your life, He doesn't want to share the credit. He wants to have all the glory and all the notoriety.

Paul summarized why He handles things this way in 2 Corinthians when he wrote, "Indeed, we personally had a death sentence within ourselves, so that we would not trust in ourselves but in God who raises the dead" (1:9). Paul's statement is a good reminder of something that is not in the Bible. It's something that gets quoted a lot and even attributed to the Bible but appears nowhere: that God will not put on you more than you can bear. That simply is not true. In fact, Paul—the apostle and chosen servant of God—wrote, "For we don't want you to be unaware, brothers, of our affliction that took place in Asia: we were completely overwhelmed—beyond our strength—so that we even despaired of life" (2 Cor. 1:8). Yes, Paul wrote that he despaired of life. He would have preferred to die than suffer. They were all "completely overwhelmed" and beyond their strength. Definitely sounds like God allowed more than they could bear.

As with Paul, and with Joseph, there is a time when God will put more on you than you can bear. This is a time when He wants to strip you of you. He wants to break you of your own self-dependence. He wants to remove your sense of self-sufficiency, your independence. God will in fact wear you down until you cry "uncle" sometimes—until you have reached a point of *total* dependence on Him.

One of the reasons some of us have not gotten off our detour is we are still too self-sufficient. We still feel like we can handle it ourselves. We think we know the right people, or have the right money, or even work the right job. We think that because of our own hookups, human abilities, talent, contacts, or even our own resources—that if we just toss a prayer on top—we can get to where we want to go.

It doesn't work that way. God doesn't work that way.

God will put more on you than you can bear when He is trying to break you down of your own independence. When God disappoints you—just when He looked like He was coming through for you—He does so in order to increase your awareness of your dependency on Him and not you. But that's good news, friend. It's good news when your human contacts can't help, or your money can't buy you out, or you find yourself thrown onto God alone. That's the best place you can be because that's when God finally gets the chance to *be* God to you.

CHAPTER EIGHT

The Plan of Detours

 In the last chapter, we looked at one clue that can let us know when we may be nearing the end of a God-ordained detour—that was when God disappoints you when it looked like you were just about to reach your destination. In this chapter, I want us to examine another hint—when God surprises you.

For two full years, Joseph sat in jail hoping the cupbearer would remember him. I'm sure after some time he assumed the cupbearer would not remember. He probably felt forgotten, overlooked by God. Waiting for that knock on the door that never came, I wonder if Joseph even bothered to keep track of the days? After that long, would you?

After that long, have you?

Are you somewhere in your life where you feel forgotten, over-looked, or even skipped by God yourself?

Have you been praying for, waiting for, and hoping for His hand of intervention but to no avail?

If that's you, then this chapter is for you. Because after preparation and development, and even breaking you, has run its course, God is ready to do to you what He did to Joseph—to surprise you.

While Joseph was locked up in prison, Pharaoh was dreaming in the palace. It wasn't a good dream, though. In fact, it was a dream that caused Pharaoh a lot of concern. So much so that he called for his magicians and all of his wise men to come interpret his dreams. But despite all his or her efforts, there was no one who could do so successfully. God didn't allow human wisdom to bring the answer to the problem. He providentially thwarted the normal processes for Pharaoh's dream interpretations because God had a job for Joe. God had someone especially created and designed for just a purpose like this. In fact, interpreting the dream was only a step toward the purpose God had for Joseph.

While Joseph sat yet another day in the jail, the wisdom of the wisest men in Egypt fell short—leaving Pharaoh at a loss for what to do next. That is, until the cupbearer spoke up. He said,

> Then the chief cupbearer said to Pharaoh, "Today I remember my faults. Pharaoh had been angry with his servants, and he put me and the chief baker in the custody of the captain of the guard. He and I had dreams on the same night; each dream had its own meaning. Now a young

Hebrew, a slave of the captain of the guards, was with us there. We told him our dreams, he interpreted our dreams for us, and each had its own interpretation. It turned out just the way he interpreted them to us: I was restored to my position, and the other man was hanged." (Gen. 41:9–13)

A lightbulb came on in the cupbearer's mind when Pharaoh's men couldn't interpret his dream. Something triggered a reminder to his own situation and the man he met in the jail, the slave. Without hesitation, Pharaoh quickly summoned for Joseph to interpret his dream. He didn't need to be told twice that there was a man who could help him. A knock came on Joseph's cell door. It opened to the light. And just as suddenly as he had been tossed into it, he was pulled out.

Some of you may call that luck, chance, or happenstance. Maybe there are a few reading this who may even call it fate. But as a believer in God, none of those words should even be in your vocabulary. What happened that day is *providence*.

Providence is the hand of God moving in the glove of history—giving a dream, having set up the dream-reader, and reminding the cupbearer about his connection from years ago. Now Pharaoh wants to meet a man he's never known and trust this man with the most delicate thoughts in his mind and heart . . . all because God is a God of time and the maneuvering of circumstances.

What happened that day is providence.

Joseph gets a jump start, a job, and a shave. It says in Genesis 41:14 that after Pharaoh sent for Joseph, Joseph shaved and changed his clothes. Having sat in the horrid environment of a dungeon for so long, it was time for a makeover. But that's exactly what God will do. When He brings you out of detour to your destiny, He cleans you up. He gets you ready. He transforms not only your soul, but everything about you. God can take off those jail clothes when He removes you from a negative reality, giving you a fresh start and a fresh face.

Finding himself before the highest ruler in the land, Joseph remembered from where he came. He remembered his dependence on God. He didn't exalt himself with positive, affirming words. Instead, Joseph revealed clearly what he learned on his detours—things like humility, dependence, and trust. The Bible says,

> Pharaoh said to Joseph, "I have had a dream, and no one can interpret it. But I have heard it said about you that you can hear a dream and interpret it."
>
> "I am not able to," Joseph answered Pharaoh. "It is God who will give Pharaoh a favorable answer." (Gen. 41:15–16)

After two years in jail, God surprised Joseph with a job. And Joseph surprised all of us with a character transformation. "I am not able to," he said plainly. "It is God." Joseph had finally matured. Joseph was prepared now for the work God had called him to do. When you are prepared for your destiny, you will be amazed at how quickly the Lord will take you there. If you ever want to do a study in the Bible, I recommend doing one on the word *suddenly*. Suddenly is when God surprises you—when He comes out of nowhere—when you couldn't have planned it or created it yourself.

Suddenly.

You think you are stuck somewhere, but then suddenly God shows you you've already arrived.

This reminds me of another airplane story that took place on a trip I had to take. This time I was flying back to Dallas from Raleigh, North Carolina, when a problem came up that caused a detour. Instead of landing in Dallas, we were rerouted to Abilene. I'll never forget sitting on the tarmac in Abilene when, suddenly, a woman passenger stood up and began talking to the stewardess. A few minutes later the stewardess went into the cockpit to talk to the captain. A few minutes after that, a crew pulled up outside of the plane with the stairs to disembark. Within moments, the door to the plane had opened and off walked the woman along with her children. Apparently Abilene had been her destination all along. They had originally been scheduled to fly to Dallas and then catch another plane back to Abilene. But as they sat there on the tarmac, they decided to ask if they could go ahead and disembark.

The crew and attendants didn't see why not—so what had originally been a detour became a destination. Suddenly.

God knows how to create situations. God knows how to take you from here, skip over there, so that you wind up here suddenly—to the place where He was taking you all along. Like the family on the plane detouring to Abilene, God can surprise you out of nowhere and take you home sooner than you ever even dreamed.

But you may be wondering how to know whether or not what is happening suddenly is really God or something else. How do you recognize a God-move as compared to something that simply happens due to life's circumstances? Oftentimes, you can recognize it by the word *twice*. In Joseph's story, we read about in Genesis 41:32 when Joseph responded to Pharaoh's question concerning what to do about his dream. He said, "Since the dream was given *twice* to Pharaoh, it means that the matter has been determined by God, and He will carry it out soon" (italics mine).

We looked at this earlier, in another chapter, but I want to bring it back up here because it is so critically important. *By two or three witnesses a thing is confirmed*, and sometimes that means God is up to something.

When you want to know if it's just chance, or Satan trying to trick you (or even just your own wishful thinking), look for a repetitious pattern. Look for *twice*.

God will always confirm His will. He will always validate His Word. And the way He did it with Pharaoh and his dream was in giving him both the cows and the corn (Gen. 41:1–7). Joseph pointed that out to Pharaoh as a way of knowing the matter had been determined by God Himself and that the thing foretold would come to pass.

Joseph could look back on his own life and see God show up in recognizable patterns. He had learned how to discern the hand of God. His humbling had come at a cost, but it was a cost that paid dividends for him and countless others in the future. One thing Joseph learned through his detours was to never get hung up on how something may appear. Whether good or bad, reality is not always what we see.

He had been given a coat of many colors early on and a vision of greatness. But he wound up in a pit, then chained behind a caravan, later sold as a slave, only to later be imprisoned.

He had been given a dungeon for his home and chains for his clothes, only to later be set free, bathed, shaved, given new clothes and a presence before Pharaoh himself in order to interpret his dream. What you see is never all there is to be seen. Joseph knew that. He knew that seven years of plenty shouldn't be any situation to set a nation at ease. He knew what the dream meant—there would be seven years of famine. And if the leaders of the country weren't wise enough to store away extra during the plenty, many would starve during the famine. Joseph learned on his detours how to view life through a long-term lens. He learned that God has a way of twisting, steering, turning, and then bringing something about suddenly and out of nowhere in order to get you exactly where you are supposed to be.

So I am challenging you today, even as you read these pages, that if you are on a detour, be certain to get in His will. Stop letting human opinion and emotion keep you on a detour longer than you need to be. Stop following the ways and methods of humanity, which contradict the ways of God. Even though I may not know how long your detour is going to be, I do know that God knows where your destiny lies and when your divine hookup is to take place. And when it does, the timing will be perfect. And, most likely, sudden.

There was a man one day who was ready to give up on God. He was tired. Life was no longer going well, and he didn't know if God was going to come through for him like he had once hoped. He had gotten to the end of his rope, the last of his hope, and wanted to give up. So he whispered to God, "I quit."

Perhaps that's you today. Perhaps that's how you feel because you can't see God, you can't hear Him. You feel like Joseph, locked up and stranded—stuck. Left to rot. Forgotten. Alone. Passed over. Even though you once held so much hope.

The man who told God he quit decided to go to the woods to have one last conversation with the Lord. "God, You disappointed me," this man said. "You've got me stuck out here, and I don't know why. I don't know how long I'm going to have to stay in this situation before my change is going to come. I'm just ready to give up—unless You do something or say something right now."

Just at that very moment, the heavens opened, and a voice spoke to the man. It said, "Look around and tell Me what you see."

The man looked around and told the voice from heaven that he saw ferns growing in a pot and also some bamboo. The voice from heaven replied, "Exactly. Now let me tell you about the fern and the bamboo." The man perked up his ears to listen intently.

"When the fern seed was planted, the ferns grew up very quickly, and they became lush and green and beautiful. But when the bamboo seeds were planted, nothing grew at all during its first year. Same thing with the second year. And the third. And the fourth. It wasn't until the fifth year that the very first small shoot of the bamboo came up."

Then the voice from heaven paused, allowing that reality to sink in. Then continued with a question, "How tall is that bamboo you are looking at?"

The man answered, "At least a hundred feet tall."

"You are right," the voice from heaven said. "And the reason bamboo is a hundred feet tall is because during the five years when you saw nothing, it was growing deep on the inside. It was growing strong, deep roots down beneath the surface where you cannot see. The reason why it was going deeper first is because it knew I had planned for it to eventually be over a hundred feet tall. It knew how high I planned to take it, and in order for it to sustain that height, it would have to grow deeper inside where no one could see anything at all."

Friend, if God is taking a long time with you on your detour, it is because He is trying to take you deeper on the inside first. He is trying to develop and strengthen you to sustain the destiny in store.

His plan for you is high. His calling for you is tall. His purpose for you will one day soar. But just as you can't build a skyscraper on a chicken-coop foundation, you can't place a divine destiny on a shallow soul. The higher your mountains, the deeper your valleys will seem. And difficult roads often lead to the most magnificent destinations.

CHAPTER NINE

The Pardon of Detours

 Two monks were on their way to a particular destination. On their way they had to cross a shallow river to get to where they were going. But when they reached the river, they ran across an elderly, heavyset woman sitting by the bank of the river. She sat there crying, and so the two monks asked her what was wrong. She proceeded to tell them that she was unable to cross the river.

She was too scared to go out in it all alone.

The two monks had sympathy for the elderly lady, and so they offered to carry her across the river. Together they picked her up and proceeded to wade into the water, gently getting themselves and her across to the other side. Once they made it to the other side, the elderly woman thanked them profusely and then went on her way. The two monks continued on to their destination. Yet as they were walking, one of the monks started to complain about the pain in his back. He mumbled, "Wow, carrying that woman across the river was really difficult. Now my back is hurting so bad."

The other monk answered his complaint with encouragement, "Well, let's keep going. You can make it."

"No," the complaining monk retorted. "I can't. I can't go on. Carrying that woman was hard. I'm hurting too bad." The monk paused and then asked his friend, "Aren't you hurting too?"

To which the other monk replied, "No, I got rid of her five miles ago."

A lot of us are failing to reach our destinations because we are still feeling loaded down by the pain of the past. The weight of yesterday continues to weigh us down today, keeping us from moving freely into tomorrow. Nothing—and I mean nothing—will hinder you arriving at your destiny like this thing called unforgiveness. Unforgiveness includes holding on to past pain, past hurts, past grudges—the weightiness of regret, remorse, and revenge. Unforgiveness is that one thing above all else that will block God's movement in your life taking you from where you are to where you are supposed to go.

When you hang on to the weight of yesterday, it will hinder the progress to tomorrow. Unforgiveness is the critical area that must be addressed if you are going to reach your destiny.

If anyone had a right to be angry, bitter, and to hold a grudge, it was Joseph. Joseph grew up in a dysfunctional family under a dysfunctional father, was dumped in a pit, sold into slavery, unjustly jailed, and then forgotten. If anyone had a right to be angry and to say, "Life is not fair!" it was Joseph. The life of Joseph fills the pages from chapter 37 to chapter 50 of Genesis, so it is obvious that God wanted us to learn from this man. He wanted us to zero in on this man's life lessons. God gave so much of the first book of the Bible to Joseph because He wanted to show us the key components to living a life of destiny. And one of those critical components Joseph had to grapple with—and that you and I will have to grapple with if we are ever going to get off of our detours and arrive at God's designed destiny for our lives—is this issue of forgiveness.

Joseph had to face it. He had to deal with it. In fact, we see this acknowledged in Genesis 50:15–17:

> When Joseph's brothers saw that their father was dead, they said to one another, "If Joseph is holding a grudge against us, he will certainly repay us for all the suffering we caused him."
>
> So they sent this message to Joseph, "Before he died your father gave a command: 'Say this to Joseph: Please forgive your brothers' transgression and their sin—the suffering they caused you.' Therefore, please forgive the transgression of the servants of the God of your father." Joseph wept when their message came to him.

Joseph's response lets us know that he had not grown emotionally cold. He had not chosen a life of cynicism in dealing with the pain he faced. He still allowed himself to feel despite the losses that had occurred in his life. He hadn't cut off the past; rather, he had learned how to view it. He had learned how to accept it in alignment with God's providence, even though the pain was obviously still there.

Forgiveness doesn't mean you no longer feel pain. Nor does it mean to forget the facts about what happened. Forgiveness means you no longer hold the situation or person hostage for the pain they caused.

Many of us are being hindered from our destiny because we are being held hostage by a leash around our souls called unforgiveness. This leash keeps jerking us back and jerking us back. We take one step forward only to be jerked backed two. Maybe it was something that happened in your childhood, or maybe it was an abusive or emotionally absent mate.

> *Forgiveness doesn't mean you no longer feel pain.*

Maybe you were forsaken, neglected, or even wrongly demoted or let go. It could be a multitude of things. Whatever it is, though, it's holding you hostage. But today, I want to see you set free.

First of all, too many of us wrongly define this concept of forgiveness. When it is wrongly defined, we never truly experience its benefits. Or we don't really know if we have done it. Forgiveness, biblically speaking, is the decision to no longer credit an offense against an offender. It is a math term, technically speaking. That's why when we hear it in the Lord's Prayer, it is specifically connected to debts. We are asking God to forgive our debts, as we forgive our debtors. It refers to an error on a calculator where two numbers have been added together wrongly, and you have to push a reset button in order to begin again.

Forgiveness has far more to do with a decision than a feeling. It is not how you feel at any given moment; it has to do with whether you have made the choice to delete the offense. You may wonder how you are to know if you have made that choice since you can't gauge your decision by your feelings. How do you know you have actually forgiven instead of simply just stated you have forgiven?

An excellent qualifying measure to help you know whether you have truly forgiven the offense and the offender is to ask yourself, "Am I still seeking revenge?" If you are seeking revenge, or payback, or if you delight in the offender's pain, or bad circumstances, then you have not yet forgiven. You have not yet released this person from the pain they have caused you.

Keep in mind, this also applies to yourself. Far too many believers live under the weight of guilt and shame and fail to forgive themselves. This can lead to destructive behavior that can span the distance from overspending to overeating to overdrinking to other methods of self-harm.

True forgiveness is setting yourself free from the bitterness of wrath and anger. If you are seeking revenge or desiring it, then forgiveness has not occurred because love "does not keep a record of wrongs" (1 Cor. 13:5). It doesn't mean you excuse it, or even pretend like it didn't happen. It also doesn't mean you ignore it.

We can see from Joseph's example that he felt great pain. He wept, even decades later. But what forgiveness *does* mean is that you have made a decision to no longer relate to the person or people, or even yourself, based on the infraction.

Two Types of Forgiveness

Forgiveness can operate on two levels. There is both unilateral forgiveness and transactional forgiveness. Unilateral forgiveness occurs when you forgive someone and yet the person has not asked for it, requested it, or even repented of what they did to you. Unilaterally means that on your own—without their involvement—you choose to grant them forgiveness.

Now, why would you grant someone forgiveness who doesn't even want it and certainly doesn't deserve it? The reason you grant unilateral forgiveness is so you can keep going. Unilateral forgiveness keeps you from being held hostage to something the other person may never get right. It could be that the offense is so small that it is not a big deal to the other person, or it's so small you don't want to bring it up. Or maybe the person who hurt you has passed away, and the opportunity for apologizing is no longer there.

This isn't a deep, personal example of needing to forgive someone unilaterally, but it is an example I think can shed light on how and why we are to do this. Some years ago, a driver of another vehicle ran into my car and sped off. It was a classic hit-and-run.

He left so quickly I was unable to get the license plate or even the make and model of the car. All I knew was that my car now had a huge dent in it and the person responsible was nowhere to be found. They didn't tell me they were sorry. They didn't offer me any insurance assistance. They just hurt my car and left.

Now it was up to me to get the dent fixed in my car, but I put it off a lot longer than I should have. I admit, I didn't want to have to fix a dent that I did not create. My stubborn frustration kept me from getting my car fixed, but it was only me who was punished as a result. The person who caused the dent never knew. That person never had to see it. I was the one who had to climb into a dented car every day, being reminded of what had happened and getting re-frustrated all over again.

I was being held hostage by a person I didn't even know. Many people are living with unforgiven dents on their souls.

Unilateral forgiveness means I forgive so that I can move on. I forgive so that I can let go. I forgive so that I can go get the dent fixed. When Stephen was being stoned to death as recorded in Acts 7, he asked God to forgive those who were killing him even in the midst of them killing him. They were still stoning him and he's forgiving them. Guess what happened when he did that? He looked up and saw heaven open up and Jesus standing on the right hand beside the Father. Why is that important to know? Because it reveals to us that forgiveness gives you a new level of access to God. It gives you a more intimate relationship with the Savior. It gives you hope in the harm and peace in the problems.

Never let the fact that the person who has hurt you has neither asked for forgiveness, nor demonstrated that they deserve it. You are to forgive so that you are no longer held hostage to an offense, person, circumstance, or loss. By an act of your decision, you release them so that you can keep going to your destiny. Nothing will hold you hostage to your detours and thus keep you from your destiny like unforgiveness.

Forgiveness is a beautiful word when you need it. It is an ugly word when you have to give it. But it is a bridge we all must cross, and it is certainly a bridge we should never burn down. Forgive others because you also need forgiveness, from God and those you offend (Matt. 6:14–15).

You may be wondering, "What about the pain?" If you forgive someone and still feel the pain—that can't be fair, right? It may not be fair but it will set you free.

In England sit magnificent churches with magnificent bells that ring loud and clear across the countryside. My wife's sister lives in England so when we visit her, I always marvel at these enormous churches and church bells. An interesting thing about the bells in the bell towers of these churches is that the bell is hung on a rope. In order for the bell to ring, it would be necessary in years gone by for someone to climb to the top of the bell tower, grab the rope, and begin to swing it. As that rope was swung, the bell would make a loud ringing sound. But do you know what would happen when the person finally let go of the rope? The bell kept ringing.

This is because the momentum of the past swings kept the bell moving. Now, the bell wouldn't hit so hard each time so the sound would ring less loudly. But it would continue to ring because sometimes it takes time for the past movements and motions to finally slow down and be still.

I want to tell you one very important thing about forgiveness. Forgiveness doesn't stop the bell from ringing. It doesn't stop the pain from showing up. But what it does do is allow you to let go of the rope. It allows you to distance yourself from the offense enough for the natural momentum of life and emotions to finally slow down and eventually be at peace. The pain will subside in time, as long as you don't pick the rope back up and ring it again.

I want you to release yourself to your destiny. I want you to let go of the offenses and wrongs done against you. Leave vengeance in the hands of God. He's far better at it than we are anyhow. Give yourself the freedom you so desperately need and so divinely deserve that will enable you to fully live out the destiny you have been created to fulfill. Forgive. Let go. Embrace that God's perfect plan involves the pain of the past, and He will bring it to His good purpose.

Then walk in the fullness of His calling for you.

CHAPTER TEN

The Pleasure of Detours

 In the last chapter we looked at the first form of forgiveness we are going to cover, which is unilateral forgiveness. Unilateral forgiveness is when you forgive someone who has not asked for it, has not demonstrated a heart of remorse, or maybe even hasn't stopped doing the offense. Unilateral forgiveness is granted so that you do not have to be held hostage to the bitter and debilitating emotions of anger, resentment, and fear.

But then there is a second form of forgiveness that I want to look at, as modeled by the life of Joseph. This is called transactional forgiveness. Transactional forgiveness occurs when there is a desire for reconciliation and repentance has taken place. It is when the person or persons who have offended you are willing to confess what was done wrong and seek to restore what has been broken. This type of forgiveness reestablishes the relationship.

Transactional forgiveness is reconciliation driven.

But transactional forgiveness needs to be proven first, depending on the severity of the offense.

Joseph's brothers wanted to be forgiven. They expressed their remorse to Joseph, but Joseph didn't take their word for it. A person can always say, "I'm sorry," and not mean it. A person can apologize due to a situation they are in, or just to try and get past the offense or its consequences. The words alone don't carry the weight that actions will reveal. It is wise for confessions to be tested to see whether they are true repentance, which is exactly what we see Joseph doing in Genesis 42. He gives his brothers a test to see if their hearts have changed from the years before when they meant him harm due to their own jealousy. This is the test:

> "This is how you will be tested: As surely as Pharaoh lives, you will not leave this place unless your youngest brother comes here. Send one from among you to get your brother. The rest of you will be imprisoned so that your words can be tested to see if they are true. If they are not, then as surely as Pharaoh lives, you are spies!" (vv. 15–16)

This test wouldn't be the only test Joseph would put them through, either. Later he put a cup in Benjamin's bag to make it look like he stole it in order to see if the brothers would throw Benjamin under the bus, or if they would try to defend him in order to return their father's newest "favorite son" home. These tests, which the brothers passed, proved they had really matured and repented of their previous evil ways. This is why the Bible says we are to see the "fruits of repentance." Fruit is something you and I can see, touch, and taste. It's visible. Words only go so far. Repentance must be a change of action for it to be real.

Granted, all relationships cannot be restored. Some can only be restored to a certain point. But in transactional forgiveness, some amount of restoration is sought. You seek to reboot the relationship as much as the situation will allow. This is a both-sides reality, too. It's not just the offended standing there asking to see the fruits of the offendee. Both sides need to demonstrate that repentance and forgiveness have taken place.

I see this far too often in counseling married couples—when one person will repent of an offense and be legitimately sorry, and the other person will offer forgiveness but in words only. Over the next days, weeks, and even months, the offended party withholds affection, offers biting words, or maintains a suspicious posture. They may even go to their friends and tell the negative situation to others in search of sympathy or shared outrage. But Joseph's story and the life he modeled for us show us what it means to truly forgive. There are several verses to this story, but let's read them all together so we retain the context for Joseph's actions:

> Then Joseph could no longer keep his composure in front
> of all his attendants, so he called out, "Send everyone away
> from me!" No one was with him when he revealed his

identity to his brothers. But he wept so loudly that the Egyptians heard it, and also Pharaoh's household heard it. Joseph said to his brothers, "I am Joseph! Is my father still living?" But they could not answer him, for they were terrified in his presence.

Then Joseph said to his brothers, "Please come near me," and they came near. "I am Joseph, your brother," he said, "the one you sold into Egypt. And now don't be worried or angry with yourselves for selling me here, because God sent me ahead of you to preserve life. For the famine has been in the land these two years, and there will be five more years without plowing or harvesting. God sent me ahead of you to establish you as a remnant within the land and to keep you alive by a great deliverance. Therefore it was not you who sent me here, but God. He has made me a father to Pharaoh, lord of his entire household, and ruler over all the land of Egypt.

"Return quickly to my father and say to him, 'This is what your son Joseph says, "God has made me lord of all Egypt. Come down to me without delay. You can settle in the land of Goshen and be near me—you, your children, and grandchildren, your sheep, cattle, and all you have. There I will sustain you, for there will be five more years of famine. Otherwise, you, your household, and everything you have will become destitute."' Look! Your eyes and my brother Benjamin's eyes can see that it is I, Joseph, who am speaking to you. Tell my father about all my glory in Egypt and about all you have seen. And bring my father here quickly."

Then Joseph threw his arms around Benjamin and wept, and Benjamin wept on his shoulder. Joseph kissed each of his brothers as he wept, and afterward his brothers talked with him. (Gen. 45:1–15)

This overview of Joseph's actions and reactions in the presence of those who had almost cost him his life is remarkable. It sheds light on so many facets of forgiveness, one being how to know if you have truly forgiven someone yourself.

Here is how you can know that you have truly forgiven someone. For starters, *you don't bring other people into the situation that have nothing to do with the sin.*

Notice how Joseph asked everyone else to leave the room before he began talking to his brothers about what they had done. You can always tell when a person who says they have forgiven someone actually has not forgiven them—*they will gossip.* They will involve people in the problem or the knowledge of the problem who have nothing to do with the problem. They include people who can't even fix the problem. This is because they are seeking revenge, not forgiveness. In addition, they are promoting the sin of gossip.

Authentic forgiveness does not bring people into situations and conversations who have nothing to do with it. Joseph left the Egyptians outside. He didn't seek to embarrass or humiliate anyone. He didn't seek to have sympathetic ears from other people.

He didn't find comfort in numbers supporting his side. He merely removed the people who weren't a part of what was going on and addressed the issue himself.

A second way you can know you have truly forgiven someone is when *you seek to make the offender feel at ease with you.*

Joseph called his brothers to come closer to him. Usually when you are still carrying a grudge against someone, you like to stay as far away as you can. If they walk into the room, you walk to the other side. If they sit at a table, you choose the chair farthest away. Joseph did neither. Rather, he asked his brothers to come near. Can you imagine asking someone who has significantly wounded you to come near?

That thought alone may cause you pain or fear. But true forgiveness creates a space where the offender who has repented can come freely and feel safe.

A third way you can discern that you have truly forgiven someone is that *you will try to help the offender to forgive himself or herself as well.* Notice back in the passage we looked at earlier that Joseph told his brothers not to be worried or angry with themselves for what they did to him. They were obviously upset over what they had done and regretted it. But once they had passed Joseph's test to know whether their repentance was authentic, he wanted them to forgive themselves as well. Joseph didn't heap guilt on top of the guilt they already felt. In fact, he tried to shovel the guilt off of them so they could stand up tall and breathe freely as well.

How was Joseph able to do that? It goes back to his view of God's providence. We catch this when he tells them not to be angry that they sold him there. In the very next breath he reminds them that God sent him there. They may have sold him, but God intentionally used that to send him. It was God's will for him to go. They were but pieces of a complex puzzle in the divine providence of the Lord.

When you have the view of God that He can even use the mess to take you to your destiny, it enables you to help the guilty people forgive themselves. God used their wrong actions to promote you to where He wanted you to be. But if you don't have that view of God, you will continue to seek your own revenge.

There is one more thing Joseph did that can help us understand and recognize true forgiveness in ourselves and in others. He told his brothers to go home and tell their father that his son Joseph was okay. What he didn't say here is actually more revealing than what he did. He *didn't* tell his brothers to confess to their father what they had done. He *didn't* send a note to his dad telling on them and ratting his brothers out. Rather, Joseph protected them from further pain and shame. The reason he was able to do this was because he had truly forgiven them.

Friend, if you are holding on to a tit-for-tat mentality, or if you are wanting someone to feel and live under the shame of what they have done, you could be blocking God's movement of you to your destiny. The Lord says that vengeance is His, and when we try to seek it ourselves, He allows us. Our vengeance pales in comparison to what the Lord can truly do, and in fact usually winds up only harming us.

When we fail to forgive, God also allows us to remain stuck on the detour of development toward maturity, faith, and letting go. And He will allow us to remain there until we finally get it. Until we finally pass the test. Until we finally mature to the point of trusting in God's providential care.

Keep in mind, forgiveness never means skipping an offense or ignoring it. Joseph didn't pretend what his brothers had done never happened. He brought it up out in the open. "Ya'll sold me here," is what he would have said if he lived in Texas like me. "Ya'll did this, and you did it to cause harm." But just because he brought it up didn't mean he continued to harbor ill feelings connected to it. Joseph knew that whatever happened to him had to pass through God's fingers first. So he was able to acknowledge the reality of past pain yet simultaneously reference present redemption.

Helps on the Path of Forgiveness

What Joseph went through was deep.

Betrayal.

Abandonment.

Lying.

Accusation.

Drudgery.

And so much more.

But there were things that God brought into Joseph's life that helped him to forgive. No, what happened to him wasn't right and it wasn't fair, but the Lord gave him grace along the way. The Lord set him up with fertile soil to forgive because the Lord provided for Joseph in ways that truly mattered.

In Genesis 41:50–52, we gain some insight into what some of these things were:

> Two sons were born to Joseph before the years of famine arrived. Asenath daughter of Potiphera, priest at On, bore them to him. Joseph named the firstborn Manasseh, meaning, "God has made me forget all my hardship in my father's house." And the second son he named Ephraim, meaning, "God has made me fruitful in the land of my affliction."

Joseph may have lost his first family, but God gave him a new one. His original family may have messed him up, but his new family brought him good. We know this because of the names he gave his sons. One was named Manasseh, which meant that God had caused him to forget all of his troubles. The other was named Ephraim, meaning God had made him fruitful in the very place he had once been afflicted.

The way Joseph kept reminding himself of how far God had brought him and that he was no longer held hostage to his old family and his old pain was in the names of his kids. Every time Joseph called to Manasseh—whether for dinner, to correct him, or send him to school—he was literally saying, "God has helped me to forget—God has helped me to forget—God has helped me to forget—God has helped me to forget!" Joseph named that child exactly what he needed to be reminded of from God.

But you may ask, "How can I forget what they did to me?" Let's get this straight for starters; Joseph didn't ever forget what they did. He later told them what they did. What Joseph forgot was the pain. He no longer lived under the pain. Yes, he remembered his old family, who they were and what they had done. But how he felt about what they had done was different. As you move from your past to your destiny, look for the Manasseh in your life. Look for what the Lord is giving to you to help you to forget the pain of the past. You can overcome the pain.

But one way God helped Joseph overcome the pain is found in the name of his second child, Ephraim. As we looked at earlier, *Ephraim* meant "God has made me fruitful in the land of my affliction." Ephraim reminded Joseph that God was blessing him right where he was right then. See, if you get so locked into the past that you fail to see the goodness of God in the right now, you will stay stuck in unforgiveness.

God has a way of blessing you exactly where you experienced the pain the most. Joseph said that "in the land of my affliction" he had been made fruitful. God didn't move him to a new place and a fresh start. No doubt Joseph would have seen Potiphar and even Potiphar's wife from time to time. The very people who left him to rot in jail had to watch Joseph rise to second-in-command. God has a way of preparing a table before your enemies and making them your footstool.

Even though you may have had a very bad yesterday, God knows how to give you a brilliant today. Look for the Ephraim He is putting on your path and in your life. When you give birth to both Manasseh and Ephraim and you call their names every day, it will help you release the pain from the past. It won't excuse the pain, but it will release it. You can forget. You can become fruitful, even in the very place or with the very people you didn't expect to ever be. In every location, job, situation, or family you never thought you'd have.

That's the power of forgiveness. Forgiveness crosses you over to the supernatural realm.

The reverse of that is true as well. Unforgiveness blocks you from the supernatural realm.

Since we all need forgiveness, to fail to give it to someone else actually blocks you from receiving relational forgiveness from God. *Forgiveness* is a beautiful word when you need it. It is an ugly word when you have to give it. But we all need both.

Friend, God will recycle your pain. He will recycle it and transform it into His purpose. I promise because He promises. You have a providentially sovereign God who can overrule and overturn what has happened to you.

He can bring you to a fulfilling, satisfying, joy-filled destiny not only in spite of what has been done to you but because of it.

CHAPTER ELEVEN

The Providence of Detours

 One of the main concepts we should avoid is the concept of luck (or luck's siblings: chance, fate, and happenstance). We regularly use the word *luck* in our everyday conversations. I know we sometimes use it innocently because we have heard it so much. But unfortunately it has not only found its way into our vocabulary but also into our mentality. Because this is so, we begin to view things from a vantage point of luck rather than divine providence.

We talk about being lucky. We call someone a lucky dog. We ask people to wish us luck. We talk about clean luck, lady luck, tough luck, good luck, bad luck, blind luck, rotten luck, lucky stars, and lucky charms. Luck is the concept of seeing events as random things that happen that affect one's life, fortune, future, or lot in life. It is that inanimate force that just sort of shows up unexpected, unanticipated—for either our benefit or our harm. And far too many of us embrace this mentality as a primary way of thinking.

Some go so far as having symbols to reflect our dependency on luck. Like the rabbit foot hanging from the rearview mirror. Now, keep in mind, this is a rabbit that was so unlucky that he couldn't even keep his own foot. But our desire to have this force—that we cannot grab, hold onto, count on, or even actually embrace— dominates much of our thinking. We want this force with us. We want to have the luck of the draw. But when you look upon luck, you have gazed upon an idol. Whenever you or I look to something, someone, or some force other than God Himself to work things out for us, that thing becomes an idol. It becomes a tool used by Satan to move your faith, hope, and trust away from God and toward chance.

Detours are disappointing. Detours are annoying. Oftentimes detours are even confusing. But too many disappointed, annoyed, and confused people today are trying to luck their way to their destiny rather than seeking what God is doing in the detour to get them there. They are hoping that if they just run into enough posi- tive forces, this will somehow produce an amorphous concept that will bring about life the way they want it to be.

Joseph didn't visualize his way out of the prison. There is no account of him meditating his way out or using positive affirma- tions to escape. The Bible doesn't tell us he sat there in jail repeating over and over again, "I am a free man, I am a free man, I am a free man."

Now, positive thinking encourages the mind and the spirit, and it is a healthy thing to do. But when you put your faith in the basket of your own mind's power to work out your destiny, you've set yourself up as an idol as well.

What we read about Joseph's time in jail focuses more on God than it does on Joseph. It tells us:

- the Lord was with Joseph (Gen. 39:21, 23)
- the Lord extended kindness to him (v. 21)
- the Lord gave him favor (v. 21)
- the Lord made everything he did successful (v. 23)

It was God who got Joseph out of jail.

It was God who got Joseph a job.

It was God who showed restraint in moving too soon while Joseph's character was being shaped.

It was God who saw the end from the beginning and orchestrated all that was necessary to take Joseph on the detours that led him straight to a destiny of epic proportions. In fact, when Stephen reviews the life of Joseph in the book of Acts, he gives the secret of his success when he says, "But God was with him" (Acts 7:9).

It was God who arranged the circumstances always and ultimately into Joseph's favor. But the word we use when we refer to God's sovereign control and arrangement of life is not luck. It is another word—a word punctuated by truth and postulated by accuracy. That word is *providence*. Providence is the hand of God in the glove of history.

Providence is one of the most important things you need to know in your Christian experience. The first most important thing, of course, is the gospel. You need to know how to come to faith in Jesus Christ for your eternal destiny through the forgiveness of your sins. That's the most important thing to know.

But following the truth of salvation—the second most important thing you must know in your Christian life—is this concept of providence. First Timothy 6:15 reminds us that God is the ruler over all and brings everything about in His perfect timing. We read, ". . . which He will bring about at the proper time—He who is the blessed and only Sovereign, the King of kings and Lord of lords" (NASB).

> *But following the truth of salvation—the second most important thing you must know in your Christian life—is this concept of providence.*

God's sovereignty means that He is the absolute ruler, controller, and sustainer of His creation. He is the One who has the final say-so. Nothing, absolutely nothing, sits outside of God's sovereignty. There are no events over which He does not rule. There are no situations that happen which He does not either create or allow.

Your boss does not have the last say.

Your mate does not have the last say.

Your parents do not have the last say.

Your health does not have the last say.

Even you do not have the last say. God created this world and all that is within it, and He rules over all.

Providence is a word that expresses one of the key ways God demonstrates His sovereignty in connection with His intentional arrangement of people, circumstances, and events to achieve His sovereign purposes. Sovereignty is God's rule. Providence is how God uses that rule to integrate, connect, attach, detach, arrange, and hook things up to facilitate His purposes. The Bible is clear that God does all things "after the counsel of His will" (Eph. 1:11 NASB). Scripture states unmistakably that God's plans cannot be thwarted. So in light of this truth, one reality that cannot ever exist is the simultaneous existence of sovereignty and luck. The two can never comingle. When there exists a sovereign God who controls all things, you cannot also at the same time have random events (luck) that shape things. One excludes the other.

What you may feel is luck or call luck is never luck. Just as darkness cannot abide where there is light, luck cannot exist within the rule of a sovereign, providential Creator God.

Throughout this book we have seen that Joseph's life contained many ups and downs. He is dressed in a coat of many colors one day and naked in a pit the next day. He's got a great job one day and is accused of rape the next. He is in a prison, forgotten by someone he helped one day, and shaved, washed, and standing before Pharaoh in the palace the next.

Joseph's life may feel like a roller coaster on many different levels. If we were to use the concept of luck, it would appear that this is a man of both great and bad luck. But when we understand the concept of providence, we know that all things were put in place *to work together for good* in Joseph's life—all things (Rom. 8:28).

What may have felt unlucky one day was actually God fulfilling His purpose in moving Joseph forward to his destiny. We don't know when Joseph learned this truth along his detours, but we do know that he learned it at some point. We know this later on in his life by his response to his brothers—the ones who had tossed him for death in the pit.

In one of the most profound and eloquent personal statements of all time, Joseph made it clear he understood providence, "As for you, you meant evil against me, but God meant it for good in order to bring about this present result, to preserve many people alive" (Gen. 50:20 NASB). In other words, God did this on purpose. What looked like an unlucky day was actually God fulfilling His purpose to bring Joseph to his destiny.

Friend, if you ever get providence—the subset of sovereignty—understood, you will begin to view all of life differently. You will begin to rest when you used to fret. You will begin to breathe easily when you used to worry. You will begin to give thanks when you used to be filled with bitterness or regret. To fully live out the victorious Christian life and experience the abundance Jesus Christ died to provide, you must live and look at the events of your life through the lens of providence.

I don't know if you are an expert in the area of geometry, trigonometry, algebra, or even basic fractions. But you can bet your bottom dollar about one thing: these all rest on one simple principle—that one plus one equals two. If you don't get the fundamentals of mathematics right, as the foundation for all else, you will never be able to make sense of the more complicated things, such as geometric calculations. All of the complexities of math fit firmly on the foundation.

Life may feel like trigonometry sometimes. It may feel like a difficult geometric proof. Things can get so complicated that they simply don't add up. But if you start with the foundation that God is sovereign, and in His sovereignty He providentially arranges all things to accomplish His goal, then you have the foundation upon which to properly solve the complexities life sends your way. What you, I, and others may look at as random events, chance encounters, or arbitrary connections are actually orchestrated events in both the purpose and plan of God. Let me put it another way— this mysterious thing called providence means that God is sitting behind the steering wheel of history. Sometimes He has us on the main highway. Other times it's down a back alley. Sometimes it looks like we are going the wrong way on a one-way street. But whatever the case, God's intentions are immaculate, and His plans are providential.

Not all detours occur on the major thoroughfares of life, and God's providence isn't only connected to the major things that happen to us. We may recognize His hand in the big things more easily, but the Lord is intimately involved in the small things as well. Sovereignty is so complete, and providence so intricate, that it is delicately woven through every detail of life. Matthew 10 tells us that God even knows the very hairs on your head and if you lose one. He knows every sparrow that falls out of a tree. It's easy to see the devil in the details sometimes, but what would help our perspective and our responses to life would be to recognize that God is in them all the more. In fact, the devil may be bad, mean, and wanting to hurt someone. But even the devil had to ask permission before he laid a hand on Job's situation. The devil is on a leash—God's leash, under God's sovereign hand. Joseph's brothers, and even the devil, may have thought they were thwarting the vision Joseph had had regarding his great position in his dream as a teen. But what was meant by them for evil was used by God for good.

What may come as a shock to you does not shock God. Sovereignty means God never says, "Oops, I missed that one." He doesn't say that because He is in control of the big things to the small, so nothing surprises Him even though they do surprise us in our finite thinking. Romans 11:33 reminds us that God's ways are "unsearchable." You can't Google His providence or plans. You can't go to your computer and type in the words "God's ways for my life" and come up with the details of how He is doing what He plans to do with you. God's ways are beyond our ability to figure out.

So don't be surprised when He just doesn't make sense. He is not supposed to. His ways are not our ways, and His thoughts are higher than our thoughts. They are as far as the heaven is to the earth. The gap between our thinking and God's thinking is infinite. We can't figure Him out. He is the *unfigure-outable* God.

The only thing you and I can figure out is what He decides to tell us. But as a parent doesn't share all things with the children he or she is raising, God doesn't share everything with us. The way He providentially twists, tweaks, moves, maneuvers, and meanders is beyond our intellectual capacity to even understand, decipher, or discern. That's why faith is so important in following God. He asks us to trust Him because like Joseph in chains behind a camel walking through the desert, it doesn't always look the way we think life should look to get us to our dream.

It is impossible to please God apart from faith because faith is the hallmark of providence. If you are on a detour that seems to have taken you on another detour, which only rerouted you to another detour, have faith. Believe and obey. Stay in the race. Stay on the road. Stay in the car. God has a way of getting you, like He got Joseph, to the palace or the place He has destined for you.

Trust Him, you may actually be closer than you think.

CHAPTER TWELVE

The Perfection of Detours

Meant.

The word can be defined as the past participle of "to mean" which is *to intend for a particular purpose and destination.* You've probably heard someone say something they probably shouldn't have said or done something that lacked tact, but someone else tried to cover it up with, "They meant well."

What they were saying is that even though what the person said or did created a negative reality, that was not their intention. Their motives were pure.

But that was not the case with Joseph's brothers when they stripped him of his coat and dumped him in a pit. Nor was that the case when they greedily plucked him from the pit and sold him for a profit to slave traders headed to a foreign land.

Joseph's brothers meant anything but well. They meant to cause him harm. They meant to ruin his life. They meant to dethrone him from the position of importance he had come to believe he would one day hold. They meant bad. Actually, they meant evil.

But God.

Those two words are two powerful words. When you come across "but God" in Scripture, pay attention. What comes next will usually change the entire situation. Especially if "meant" is added after them.

But God meant . . .

We read, "As for you, you meant evil against me, but God meant it for good in order to bring about this present result, to preserve many people alive" (Gen. 50:20 NASB). When Joseph confronted his brothers after God had turned his situation around, he chose those words. He chose to let his brothers know that the very exact thing they had meant to cause him harm was the very exact thing God had used to bring him to his destiny. I don't want you to miss that because oftentimes when we think about God working things out for good, we think about Him working around the negative things. But in this case, God gives us an example of working directly *in* the negative thing.

Joseph's brothers meant evil. And with the very evil they used, God used that mess for good. The very same mess Joseph's brothers meant for harm is the very same mess God meant for good. That's good news if someone has ever done something intentionally to hurt you. That's comforting knowing that even the evil people have intended toward us is used by God for good, when we surrender under His plan. Providence includes using the negative to produce a positive. God's sovereignty does not only include good things, but it also includes the bad and what other people mean for harm.

This might be a curveball in the way you view hurtful situations, but here is how it works.

Since God is sovereign, nothing happens outside of His rule. But within His rule He has created freedom. Freedom means you get to choose. There is no freedom without choice. You are free to say "yes" or to say "no." You are free to go or you free to stay. God created freedom. But how can a sovereign God control everything while simultaneously creating freedom? Let me try to explain it through an illustration of football.

In football, there are sidelines and goal lines, which serve as sovereign boundaries. These do not move. You can't negotiate them. You can't make them wider or narrower. These are fixed standards with which the game of football is played. If you step over a sideline, you are out of bounds. Period. Because that is a boundary.

But within those boundaries teams are free to run their own plays. They can call a good play or a bad play. They can gain yardage or they can lose ground. They are free to play within the boundaries established by the game.

God is sovereign in the boundaries He has set for us. But He allows freedom within those boundaries that give us the choice to do good or to do bad. To be right or to be wrong. To intend evil or to intend well. While freedom doesn't *cause* evil, it does *allow* for it.

Yet He limits how free He lets us go within His providential connection of all things. Providence is God either causing or allowing things to happen for His purposes. That is not to say He endorses evil or sin, but rather He redeems it. He redeems the bad intention of someone who may have hurt you on purpose by intervening in you to twist that thing to work for your good. His merciful hand will use what was meant for harm—for good. He will even use evil to accomplish His purpose, as we have seen with Joseph.

Scripture tells us that God even made Pharaoh's heart hard so that Pharaoh would chase the Israelites out of Egypt. He took the evil in Pharaoh's heart and allowed it to be even more evil in order to fulfill His purpose of delivering His people from that place. God is so good at His providential work of hooking stuff up and arranging things to accomplish His will that He can even use the devil to help a brother out. He can even use someone who means you harm to take you, mold you, develop you, strengthen you, or redirect you to your purpose and your destiny. God even uses Satan to accomplish this as in the case of Job, Peter, and even Jesus.

Despite the rise of smartphones, people still wear watches. I still wear a watch even though I could look at my phone anytime I wanted to see what time it is. But it's a habit when you want to know what time it is to look at your wrist. You look at the face of your watch because that is what will show you the time. But the only reason you can see the time on the face of your watch is because of what is underneath it. If you were to open up your watch, you would see a myriad of tiny, itsy-bitsy particles and pieces interconnected and interrelated somehow. These pieces turn together in just the right order so that you can see what time it actually is on the outside of the watch. But you can't tell the time by looking at the gears.

Life is a lot like a watch. Sometimes we see the face; sometimes we see tiny individual pieces. But we never see everything. There is so much more happening behind the scenes, underneath the hood, behind the curtain in places and in people that we could never see. When you are dealing with the providence of God, you never see all there is to see. In fact, the things you do see often don't connect. It might look like there are parts that don't seem to relate to one another at all. That's because God is always doing more than one thing at a time; He's doing fifty million things at the same time.

Sometimes, when we can't see what He's doing, we feel like He isn't doing anything at all. Sometimes it looks like God is sleeping when He should be awake. Or His phone is busy, and He can't hear our prayers at all. Sometimes, if we admit it, it looks like He's gone on vacation and left us on a detour for way too long.

It may even seem like more than just a vacation. For Joseph, if we were to do the math, it would be twenty-two years before he reached his destiny. From the time he was seventeen years old to the time he stood before his brothers with them kneeling before him as he had seen in his vision, twenty-two years had come and gone. Joseph is a true reminder that we rarely arrive at our destiny overnight.

Very few people get to God's intended purpose for their lives quickly. It takes time not only to develop you for your destiny but to develop your destiny for you. God is the master weaver, and things are rarely as they appear. That is why it is so critical to walk by faith and not by sight.

Have you ever seen an orchestra when musicians first come out and are getting ready to play? All of the instrumentalists are warming up at the same time, and it sounds like chaos. It sounds like no one on the platform even knows how to play. That is because all of the different sounds are discombobulated all over the place. There is no harmonizing taking place.

Then all of a sudden, out of nowhere it seems, a conductor walks out. He stands confidently and quietly in front of the musicians. He pulls out a small stick and raises it slightly. When he does, everyone in his or her chairs who had been playing their instruments sit up straight and look directly at him. Then when he taps the stick a couple of times and begins to wave his hand, what had once appeared to be pure chaos now makes sense. The random, disconnected tunes that had previously polluted the air suddenly turn into a beautiful, powerful harmonious song.

Friend, if you feel like your life is in chaos, with so many disjointed and disconnected noises, don't leave the concert hall before the symphony swells. Don't check out on your faith. Wait for the Conductor to appear, because when the time is just perfect, He will bring harmony to discord. He will show up and turn a disappointment into a destiny.

Not too long ago I was in my office at the church when one of our members came in for a short meeting. We were chatting for a few moments before the meeting was to take place, and, as small talk, I asked him how his job was going. I knew he had finished his master's degree not long before, and so I was curious how things were going for him.

"I just got laid off last week," he said.

"What?" I asked, shocked to hear it. This man had held this job for over five years. It had provided a stable environment for him to pursue his master's, while still taking care of his wife and daughter. But now, out of the blue, due to the economic downturn, the company he worked for was cutting back.

"Yea," he said, looking dejected. "Pastor, they cut back, and I was one of the ones removed, and I've got a brand-new baby on the way. It's just not a good time for us, as a family, to lose my job."

Trying to turn the conversation to something positive, I asked him what kinds of things he wanted to do. Maybe I knew someone to whom I could refer him.

His eyes lit up a bit and he replied, "Well, now that I've finished my master's in media from the seminary, I really hope to get into that field somehow, based on my training and my passions. But finding a job like that might take some time; so right now, I just need to get a job so I can take care of my wife and the babies."

As he spoke, I couldn't believe my ears. Because we had just experienced an employee in that exact same field resign that very week in our national ministry.

Now I should note that this is a position that has only come open *maybe* once in a decade, and here it was coming open the very week this man, who now held a degree and a desire, in the exact field he got laid off from his job.

The two men didn't know each other. There was absolutely no connection between them. One resigned. The other got laid off. And by luck—I mean, by chance—okay, by providence, God had him walk into my office for a meeting about some small project my daughter had asked him to volunteer to do the very same week the position had come open. And by this same providential God, I had been prompted to ask him how his job was going. Within a week or two, at the most, he was hired. And it's been a great fit both for us and for him.

You can call that luck, chance, or happenstance, if you want. But you wouldn't be calling it correctly. Because that was the providential hand of a sovereign God aligning all people at the exact time for the right connection to take place.

When you understand providence, you start looking to see what God is doing. You start opening your eyes to see where He is moving. You start operating on a different level of understanding when you observe the patterns of God's providential maneuvering.

If you are a baker, you know how to prepare a cake. You know that none of the individual ingredients would be all that enjoyable on their own. No one would sit down and eat a stick of butter. Nor would you scoop your hand in the sugar and put it to your mouth. You don't dig into the flour with a spoon and eat a spoonful of flour.

No one does that. And the reason why no one does that is because, on their own, each ingredient is nasty. Raw eggs are just plain nasty.

But when everything gets mixed together according to a great recipe, by a master chef, and baked in the oven, you wind up with a masterpiece. This is because all things are now working together for the good of the cake.

It may look like God has your life in bits and pieces right now. You can't possibly see how, or why, any of it could amount to much good. There doesn't appear to be a real connection to a lot going on. The delays are bitter. The disappointments leave a bad taste in your mouth. But when you allow God, in His providential care, to mix it all together according to His purposes and plan, all things will work together for our good. I promise. And the reason why I can promise is because God says so in His Word. It's probably a verse you have heard so many times that it may have somehow lost its impact, but if you will let the truth of it truly sink in, it can change your entire life.

"And we know that God causes all things to work together for good to those who love God, to those who are called according to His purpose" (Rom. 8:28 NASB). And that good will always be connected with conforming us to the image of Christ (v. 29). For God is not just concerned about our circumstantial deliverance, but more importantly, He is concerned about our spiritual development. To that end, He will use all things to work together for good.

Even those things that others may have meant for evil.

All things means *all* things.

CHAPTER THIRTEEN

The Perspective of Detours

 An employer sent out a memo to all of his employees that he was going to give them a Christmas gift. The year had been a good one, financially speaking, for the company, and so he wanted to give them a little something special. He put on the note, "Just one thing, I want everyone to make a contribution to this particular charity that I'm involved with after you receive your gift. You can make it for whatever amount you want, but you must make some contribution from your bonus to this charity. I would also like 100 percent company-wide participation."

The word went out to the employees that the employer wanted everyone to participate in contributing to the charity of his choice. But there was one employee who refused, claiming that his Christmas bonus belonged to him, and he would not contribute to the designated charity. When the owner of the company found out that this one employee refused to go along with his request, he called him into his office.

Once in his office, the employer asked if it were true that he was not going to participate in giving to the charity out of his bonus check. The employee replied, "Yes, that is correct. I'm not going to give."

"But you do understand that I was seeking 100 percent company-wide participation in this?" the boss asked.

"Yes, I understand," the strong-headed employee responded. "But I do not want to be forced to give to a charity, so I am not going to do so."

The boss leaned back in his chair, thought through his word choices carefully, and then said, "That gives me two options, then. Option number one is to convince you to change your mind so that I can have 100 percent participation in giving to this charity. Option number two is that I fire you so that I have 100 percent in giving to this charity. I will leave the choice up to you, but I will have 100 percent participation in giving to this charity."

To which the employee quickly replied, "Well, no one ever really explained it to me quite like that before. Yes, I'll give."

Perspective will bring wisdom to our whims and clarity to our choices. It gives us discernment between our detours and our distractions.

See, not everything that pulls us off the path is a divinely authored detour. Some things are distractions. They are things that keep us from our destiny but have no purpose in developing us for our destiny. These things could be people, hobbies, thoughts, or even work that is not in alignment with God's purpose in our lives. Perspective will help you gain the insight to see what is a detour designed by God and what is a distraction you simply need to muster up the courage to let go of and move on from.

Many of us are waiting for our time to come, when we will reach our full potential of our divine design, when we will reach that place God is taking us in order to bring about our greatest good, bring Him the greatest glory, and expand His kingdom the most.

Destiny involves the coming together of these three things—your *good*, God's *glory*, and the *advancement of His kingdom* through the impact on others. Only when you have the true perspective of destiny can you fully live it out. If you are not interested in God's glory or His kingdom because you are only interested in your good, then you are not ready to be connected with your destiny. God wants 100 percent participation in His kingdom agenda, but it is your choice if you participate or not.

On this journey to destiny, you can slow it down or speed it up based on how you respond to the detours God places in your life in order to develop you—and the distractions you simply need to let go.

There are many reading this book who are waiting for God to do something. You are waiting for change to come. Maybe you are in a situation in life where you are saying on a regular basis, "I didn't sign up for this."

Perhaps you didn't sign up to still be single, or walked out on as a spouse and left as a single parent.

Maybe you didn't sign up for a miserable relationship.

Or to be stuck in a job that brings you no satisfaction and barely pays your bills.

It could be that you are in a difficult health situation or lost a loved one and you are sitting there saying, "I didn't sign up for this. This is not how I wanted my life to be." Despite believing God, asking God, calling on God, and looking for God to make a move, you are still stuck wondering when you will arrive at your destiny.

If this is you, what I want you to know as a believer in Jesus Christ is that you have a destiny. And oftentimes, you are closer than you think. Pass the test. Don't throw in the towel. Respond rightly to wrong treatment. Do good. Defend the defenseless. Honor God. Grow in faith. Trust. Wait. And before you know it, your destiny suddenly will be upon you. But yes, those things are often difficult to do. So remember this: As you meander through the detours toward your destiny of living out your divine design, the thing that will allow you to keep going despite life's circumstances is having the right perspective.

Perspective is how you view something. It's like the boy who lost his contact lens and was looking for it for thirty minutes. He couldn't locate it even after all that time when his mom walked in the room and asked him what he was doing. Within a minute of looking for the contact lens, his mom had found it. "How did you find it so quickly?" the boy asked.

"We weren't looking for the same thing," his mom replied. "You were looking for a contact lens. I was looking for $150."

Big difference. And it's found in perspective.

Perspective not only affects what you see but also what you achieve. That is why it is critical to have the right perspective while pursuing your destiny. Particularly when you are on a detour.

When you are in that spot where you have not yet hit your sweet spot, you need to know how to view things. You may feel

Perspective is how you view something.

far removed from purpose, passion, and peace. But sometimes, whether you realize it or not, you are only a step away.

One of the things I dread doing is walking on the treadmill. I have never looked forward to walking on the treadmill. Walking fast and sweating while going nowhere—while covering absolutely zero territory—is not my idea of how to spend my life. I'm allergic to boredom, and boredom is just about all a treadmill has to offer me.

That's why if you ever find me on a treadmill, you will also find me watching television. So common is this setup that in nearly every fitness center in the country today, you will find televisions built into the exercise equipment or hanging nearby on the wall. This is because most people feel the same way I do. Exercise on a treadmill just isn't that much fun.

What does the television do in helping you or me exercise? It shifts our focus while we work. It gets us looking at something different from the anguish we feel at the moment. When you are focusing on television while agonizing on the treadmill, it doesn't remove or reduce the effort you are putting in, but rather it enables you to bear it better. It does so because something else has grabbed your attention and owns your perspective.

As you maneuver to your destiny, my friend, I want to share with you what will take you through these ups, downs, twists, and turns—enabling you to go up the inclines and down the paths, on the positives and through the negatives you face—so you can arrive at God's intended destination. The key to your spiritual success is *focus*.

The secret to Joseph arriving at his destiny is he refused to leave God out of the equation. While in the deepest, darkest pit of jail, the Lord was with Joseph. While serving the basest of people in the prison system, God caused all that Joseph did to prosper. While living as a slave in the house of a high official, the Lord blessed Joseph's hands.

Over and over we read in this man's story that the Lord was with Joseph. Even when Joseph finally stood before Pharaoh—and if ever there was a time for self-promotion in order to maneuver his way out of the dungeon, it was then—Joseph deferred to God in all things. "It is not me who will answer Pharaoh," he had stated as boldly as he had once told his brothers they would one day bow before him. God Himself will give Pharaoh a favorable answer (Gen. 41:16).

Every time we see Joseph, without fail, we see God as well. God was never a "sometime" God for Joseph. He wasn't a fair-weather friend or an addendum. Nothing happened in the life of Joseph that God did not allow and approve and make Himself visible within. In fact, when Joseph confronted his brothers to calm their fears regarding their unrighteousness toward him, he invokes God's name five times in summarizing God's involvement in his detour to destiny (Gen. 45:5–9). We are not told this in Scripture, but I imagine one of the reasons God was with Joseph was because Joseph was with God. Joseph didn't lose sight of God. Joseph didn't give up on the dream. Joseph didn't turn his gaze to his surroundings. The Bible tells us that blessed are those who have a pure heart because they will see God (Matt. 5:8).

Not everyone gets to see God. Not everyone is privileged to live a life of God's close and clear confirmations and directions. Not everyone experiences God's favor, whether in a difficult scenario, or a seemingly blessed one. Purity doesn't refer to perfection—it refers to the absence of distraction, otherwise known as a blemish. When your heart is open to God, your eyes will be as well.

There is an individual in our church who seems to receive more signs and confirmations from the Lord than I have ever known anyone to experience. It's almost as if this person and the Lord live like intimate friends with daily back-and-forth conversations. This person isn't perfect, but this person has a relentless purity of heart toward God like few I've ever seen. So when God speaks, it is heard. When God directs, it is seen. When God confirms, it is clear. It is like a cadence with the King Himself. As a result, God's favor is witnessed almost everywhere.

Joseph experienced a level of communication and favor with God unlike many others. But I don't believe it is because God forced Himself on Joseph. Rather, Joseph's heart purely believed the promises of God, and his perspective patterned the Lord's.

If you take God seriously, you can never be a victim to your circumstances because your circumstances wouldn't be your circumstances without God allowing it to be used to take you to your destiny. When the enemy is able to remove your consideration of God in the circumstances, particularly if it is a negative circumstance, he has succeeded in adding delays to your detours. If Satan can keep God out of the equation of your understanding, you will lose perspective on the treadmill of life and only see the sweat of the uphill climb.

God was the sum total of Joseph's life.

All through his story, God was referenced, no matter what the circumstances were. God was what the ocean is to a pebble therein—the expanse surrounding everything around the pebble. The ocean totally encompasses the pebble, as we ought to acknowledge God as totally surrounding us. Rather than pop a pill or pull out a pipe, fill yourself completely and consolingly with God. The thing that marked Joseph apart from so many others was that his life was punctuated by God's presence.

Joseph had no credentials to get where he needed to be.

He had no résumé to land him the job of saving a nation, or two, or ten from famine.

He had no personal contacts, political contacts, relational contacts, or even circumstantial contacts.

He could pull no strings or pave no paths.

He was a nobody in a foreign land, with no résumé or name to assist him. Everything that society looks for to make you a success—he had nothing of at all.

All Joseph had was God. But God was more than enough to make up for everything else he lacked.

It seems that we live in a society where so much emphasis is put on striving after what culture says you must have, be, and do in order to climb the ladder of success and influence. Society tells us we need to pile on our degrees, network, look a certain way, say and do certain things to get somewhere in life. But look at Joseph. The man was stripped of every single thing a man can be stripped of, except for one thing: his destiny. Because his destiny sat securely in the hand of God.

When your destiny is in God's hands and you are trusting God with all your heart—in spite of your circumstances, mistakes, detours, and distractions—no one can block what God has for you. You may have lost a lot in your life, but you have not lost your destiny. And if you will simply align your perspective with the Lord's, you may be closer to reaching it than you think.

God loves to flip things on a dime. He loves to operate in the surprise of "suddenlies." Because when He does, He is the only One who can get the credit and the glory.

CHAPTER FOURTEEN

The Peace of Detours

 Genesis 50:20 is often used as the hallmark card of Christianity. This one verse, possibly more than any other, summarizes the power of an almighty God to transform pain into purpose and misery into a miracle.

We quote it.

We text it.

We memorize it.

We post it on social media.

But there is something hidden within this popular verse that we sometimes fail to see. It's the order in which things occurred.

Let's look again at the verse, "As for you, you meant evil against me, but God meant it for good in order to bring about this present result, to preserve many people alive" (NASB).

There is an order that shows up in this verse that I want to point out. The reason is because if you can keep this perspective in mind in your life, you will discover the secret to facing life's challenges, disappointments, pain, and confusion head-on. You will access the power to overcome anything and to rise above what you face. Here is the order I want you to see: *Evil. God. Good.*

The verse says that Joseph's brothers meant evil. But God intervened. Then good was brought about. Whenever evil shows up and God is put in the equation, good comes out of it.

So what the enemy has to do in order to be successful in his schemes is to keep God out so that the good doesn't come about. If Satan can keep God out of the middle, he can keep evil in control as the dominant influence in that situation. But the moment you allow God into the situation and put your focus on Him, God turns evil into good.

Job found evil in his life, but when he submitted and surrendered to God, God flipped it and made it good. The people following Jesus faced hunger, but Jesus brought God into that mess, and God turned a negative reality into a miracle. Lazarus was dead. But Jesus turned a death into a resurrection.

All throughout Scripture we can see the pain and suffering of this present life transformed into life and purpose when God is brought to bear on it.

That's why God must be an integral part of your everyday existence and not just a visit here or there. God doesn't want visitation privileges with you on the weekends. He wants to be your best friend. He wants to be your partner. He wants to be your team-mate, captain, coach, general, lover, leader, and companion.

There is an interesting reality about Joseph's detour that I want to bring up here briefly, and that is Joseph was single. I won't go too deeply into what that means or the implications of it, but one thing I have noticed in pastoring over four decades is that oftentimes it is the single Christian who experiences God in a supernatural way. Perhaps this is due to what Paul argued in the New Testament that a married person has divided loyalties and attention. Whatever the case, God desires to be your spouse, whether you are single or not. He says He is a spouse to you (Isa. 54:5), but when we have other people in place, or when we tend to rely on ourselves too much, we can lose sight of the proper relationship of love God longs for us to have with Him.

If God is simply an add-on to your evening meal, a prayer before you sleep, or a box you check off on Sundays, do not look to Him to turn the evil done to you into good. God must be in the middle of all you do for this pattern to take place. Friend, I dare you to go for broke on God and discover all He can really do. Put all your eggs in His basket and watch Him show up in a way you've never experienced before.

Evil. God. Good.

You can't skip God and get to the good. Without God, you wind up with Evil. Mess. Misery.

Every pit Joseph faced took him to a new place. His brothers' jealousy was evil. It was rooted in sin. They intended him harm in stripping him and dumping him to die, later selling him to slave traders. Yet if none of that had happened, Joseph would be among the many dying of starvation decades later when the known world faced a famine.

Potiphar's wife's lust was evil. Her desire for sexual relations with Joseph was immoral. She intended him harm when she lied about him and accused him, leaving him to rot in a jail. Yet if that had not happened, Joseph would never have met the baker and the cupbearer who would one day be his bridge to bring him before the highest ruler in the land. And Joseph would have died of starvation, along with the rest of the nation, years later when food ran out.

Instead, Joseph winds up being second-in-command at the exact time in history when his wisdom, insight, strategy, and skills were most needed to bring about the literal salvation of people far and wide. You tell me how someone winds up being second-in-command in Egypt who has no political degree, no résumé, no background—my goodness, he is not even an Egyptian!

God, that's how.

God can take you places and open doors you never even dreamed possible. Oh how I wish you could see the full potential of your destiny. Oh how I wish you could see the things God longs to do for you. I wish you could know the satisfaction you can experience when you live out the plan He has for you.

Your destiny isn't determined by you getting you to your desired location in life. It isn't determined by your planning, degrees, or even your networking. Yes, God can use those things, but oftentimes He won't. Rather, He meets us in a place of obedience while still on a detour and takes us to where we need to go. God has ways to hook you up that are based on nothing tangible at all.

There is a member of our church who recently came into a dream job simply due to a phone call. Nothing more. It was a simple phone call to interview someone she had never met before on a project she was working on. She wasn't excited about this project. Nor was she excited about the phone call. But she did it out of obedience to her boss and the responsibilities of her job. Yet within minutes of the interview ending, the person being interviewed began texting her. He asked her about her background, skills—what she does. It all seemed odd to her at first, she later told me. Why would this person of his stature be asking about her skills. Doesn't he have people?

But she answered him. And literally within days he had hired her for an influential role that proved to be a perfect fit for her passion, skills, and destiny. Talk about sudden! Later, he would share how this came about.

He said he had been praying for a person to fill this role, and when he heard her voice, he knew she was the one.

You can't go to school for that. You can't get on LinkedIn for a connection like that. You can't even submit a résumé for that. God, and God alone, knows how to connect you with your destiny when the time is right. And He doesn't need much to do it. A voice on a phone will do.

Joseph wound up second-in-command in Egypt because of a coat he never even asked to have. Not only that, he wound up with the authority and ability to move his whole family to Egypt and enable them to have plenty to eat during a time of worldwide famine. God used one mess after another mess and one situation after another situation to bring him to his destiny.

Success is not what you have; success is Who you have.

Now, I'm not dismissing the value of education, preparation, dedication, or pursuit. But what I am saying is that all those things, without God, will not lead you to your destiny. None of those things without God can still get you there. Knowing that is true, where do you want to put the majority of your time, talent, treasures, attention, focus, and hope?

Success is not what you have; success is Who you have.

Some of you are waiting on God to turn things around all the while God is waiting on you. Some of you are asking God to intervene in your situation while He's asking you—like Joseph—to live out the favor He has already given to you. Be obedient in the pit, in the prison, in the chains—as the slave. Had Joseph opted for sulking in jail rather than receiving the favor of God and rising to a position of influence, he would never have been in a position to interpret the dreams of the baker and the cupbearer.

If you want to get to your destiny, be fruitful where you are now. Wherever you are now, work faithfully, serve willingly, submit joyfully, and honor God fully. While God is designing a destiny especially for you, live obediently where He has currently placed you. You never know how He will use a conversation where you are at now to take you to your very own happily ever after. God is the master connector.

Friend, I don't know what the enemy is doing to discourage you. But I'm sure it's clever, consistent, and crafty. Yet when God lets you lose, it's only to show you how to win. Therefore, never be satisfied with settling simply because the wait is too long or the road too hard. Be like that beach ball in the swimming pool—so filled with the power of God's Spirit that no matter how deep the ball is pushed down beneath the water, it only uses that as a springboard to pop back up even higher than before.

I understand that when you are down, the tendency is to give up on God. But let me challenge you to change your perspective.

The more miserable things get, the more aggressive you should go after Him. It's easy to praise God in the sunshine, but if it's storming in your life right now, and darkness is all you see, force your praise from your mouth. Run to Him in the dark. Be like Jacob who wrestled all night long and demand your blessing before He lets you go.

And lastly, be patient. We will talk about this more in the next two chapters, but let's start on it briefly here.

It was thirteen years from the time Joseph was sold as a slave to the time he stood before Pharaoh.

It was twenty-two years before he connected with his brothers again.

It took Moses forty years before God got him to the place He needed him to be in order to fulfill his destiny of setting His people free.

It took Noah a hundred and twenty years before God fulfilled His promise to him.

It took Jesus thirty years as God on Earth before He even began His public ministry.

Detours take time. Development takes time. But if I know one thing at all, it is this: destinies are worth the wait. So just because you may have to yield to a lot of inconvenience, or just because you have to go through a period in life where things do not look to be working out like you thought they should—it doesn't mean you will not get there. Too many of us want a microwave God when God is often much more of a Crock-Pot. He wants to let that stuff bubble, sit, and simmer until it's cooked through and through. Until the transformation occurs fully in your life.

Now, here is one way you can know that God is working on your behalf. It won't be because there are no challenges. It won't be because nothing is ever wrong. You will know that God is working on your behalf because every time it looks like you are going down, you bounce back.

Have you ever seen someone who manages to come through trial after trial, discouragement after discouragement? Take a note of that person if you do. That is a person with the hand of God's destiny all over him or her. That is a person whose faith is firmly rooted in the living God. That is a person who understands and believes that when evil rears its ugly head, God can turn it around for good.

When I was a boy growing up in Baltimore, my daddy bought me a balloon punching bag. I loved that balloon punching bag, because no matter what I did to it, it kept bouncing back.

I'd hit it, then BOOM! It'd hit the floor.

But then, BAM! It'd bounce back up.

I'd hit it again, BOOM! It'd knock down to the floor.

But then, BAM! It'd be right back up.

Over and over and over I'd hit this bag, and over and over and over it would bounce up for more. One time I even kicked that punching bag. But it still popped right back up.

The reason that balloon punching bag kept coming back for more was because there was a weight at the bottom that was heavier than the air at the top. That way, no matter what I did to it up top, down below determined where things wound up.

I don't know what these next days, months, or even years hold for you. I don't know if you will face more detours, more challenges, or more pain. But what I can guarantee you is that somewhere down the line Satan or circumstances will give you a hit—BOOM! Some trial or trouble will knock you down. BAM! Because that's life. It happens to all of us, especially when we face an enemy who wants nothing more than to get our eyes off of God when He wants to take you deeper.

In fact, the devil may even give you several punches all at once—*boom, boom, boom, boom, BOOM*! But, friend, if you are resting on the right foundation, you will come back. If you are rooted in the right foundation, you will bounce back. If you are tied to the solid weight of a Holy God, you will stand upright again. Nothing anyone can do to you can keep you down when God is your counterbalance.

Let Him be the stability of your days as He leads you to your destiny.

CHAPTER FIFTEEN

The Patience of Detours

 If the truth be told, and we were all being totally frank, most of us do not like to wait.

Sure, we can pretend that we are patient here or there—and act all spiritual—but deep down inside, patience is a virtue that is often difficult to come by. Particularly if we are waiting for something we want to change or for something we need to improve and get better. Waiting can be a frustrating experience.

Have you ever been at a red light that won't seem to ever go to green? You feel stuck. Trapped. Held back from where you want to go. The circumstance in front of you simply won't let you move forward. Or, how about being stuck behind a slow-moving vehicle on a narrow road that won't provide room to pass?

Perhaps you've sat in the waiting room of a doctor's office, and they just keep calling everyone else's name except yours. What's worse is when you are in an emergency room, and you are in pain. Yet, they are telling you they will get to you when they can. They are literally forcing you to wait while you are frightened and in pain.

How about this? Have you ever been on the phone, and the person on the other line asks you to hold and then plays music? We all have, at some point or another. It may only be minutes, but it can feel like hours as you sit and listen to music that really should never be called music at all.

All of those kinds of waiting are inconvenient. All of them try our patience. They can strip the smile straight off our face. But really the worst kind of waiting there is comes when you or I have to wait on God.

When God forces you to wait for things to get better in your life, for things to improve, for your change to come. It is in these times when it feels as if nothing is happening, and God has put your life in neutral. Your motor is running, but the wheels aren't turning. That can cause the most pain.

God never seems to be in a hurry when we are, does He? He's like the proverbial parent who insists on cooking and eating breakfast before the Christmas presents can be unwrapped. We wonder, "What gives, God? Don't You see how much I want to get to my destiny? I'm here. I'm ready. Why are You taking so long?"

It's like the boy who was praying, "Dear Lord, I need the snow. I want it to snow. It's winter. It's Christmas. I want it to snow." Day after day he prayed for snow. But still there came no snow. "God," the boy continued after weeks, "You don't want me to become an atheist, do You? Because I'm asking for snow but there is no snow!"

Sometimes it seems that God takes so long that you can begin to wonder if believing in Him is even reasonable. You begin to wonder if it's even worth the effort. What's the upside to this thing called faith, God? You've got me waiting too long for my destiny, my mate, my healing, my hope . . . you name it. It's taking too long, and I'm beginning to wonder if I should even keep waiting at all.

You talk to Him.

You pray to Him.

You made a prayer closet.

It did no good.

You go to church.

You still feel empty and stuck.

You worship, but nothing has changed.

After a while you begin to feel that the relationship is too one-sided. Then, when things get even worse, you may even consider pulling back. Withholding worship, prayer, devotion—because it just doesn't make much sense anymore.

The clock keeps ticking. The years keep changing. The calendar keeps moving. God keeps delaying His response.

Most of us are like Habakkuk in times like these when he cries out to the Lord, "How long, O Lord, will I call for help, and You will not hear?" (Hab. 1:2 NASB). God's response doesn't offer much by way of comfort. We see it in the next chapter:

Then the LORD answered me and said, "Record the vision and inscribe *it* on tablets, that the one who reads it may run. For the vision is yet for the appointed time; it hastens toward the goal and it will not fail. Though it tarries, wait for it; For it will certainly come, it will not delay." (Hab. 2:2–3 NASB, emphasis mine)

God promises the prophet the vision will not fail. But He also lets him know "it tarries." He also reminds him to "wait for it." He doesn't tell him how long. He doesn't give him a sign. He just says it will one day come, so wait.

It's like fishing in a pond where nothing seems to bite. You can stand there or sit there for hours, tossing line after line into the water. Hooking worm after worm onto the line. Ultimately, it may feel like you are no longer fishing—you are just cruelly drowning worms. Waiting for your destiny—for your change, for your hope to happen—can feel like drowning sometimes. Your dreams are drowning. Your desires are drowning. Your thoughts are drowning. Your opportunity is drowning. Nothing seems to be hooking onto the hope you toss out time and time again. And in your private moments—those moments alone that only you and God share— you may even feel like bailing. Pulling the line out of the water and just walking away.

Holding patterns in life are just as frustrating, just like holding patterns on a flight. You just circle and circle and circle and circle. And your soul loses the hope to even hope for something different. Yet over and over again in the Bible we are told to "wait on the

LORD." It is not something that appears once or twice. The phrase and concept to "wait on the LORD" is a frequent occurrence. In Psalm 130:5–6 (NASB) it says, "I wait for the LORD, my soul does wait, and in His word do I hope. My soul waits for the LORD more than the watchmen for the morning; Indeed, more than the watchmen for the morning."

"More than the watchmen for the morning." Think about that. If you've even known or seen a watchman—or even been one—morning can't come too soon. Yet it's like the watched pot that never boils; . . . it delays and delays and delays. This is how the psalmist says he waits. This is how we are to wait as well.

With anticipation.

With hope.

With longing.

With expectation.

With desire.

With faith and obedience.

These things, and more, dissipate doubt. It dissolves despair. As we read in Psalm 27:13–14 (NASB), "I would have despaired unless I had believed that I would see the goodness of the LORD in the land of the living. Wait for the LORD; be strong and let your heart take courage; yes, wait for the LORD."

In Lamentations we find a benefit to waiting well, "The LORD is good to those who wait for Him, to the person who seeks Him. It is good to wait quietly" (Lam. 3:25–26). God is good to those who wait well. But what does it mean to wait well? How should we wait on the Lord in such a way that we receive His goodness at the end of the day? Does it mean to sit in a rocking chair and hope something better happens? Does it mean to stop talking altogether? When have we prayed enough? When have we done enough? When are we supposed to do something?

None of those questions has an exact answer for each and every situation. The answer can vary depending on the situation. But, overall, to wait on the Lord means not to go outside of God to fix the issue you are waiting for. To not "pull an Abraham" and go find yourself a "Hagar" to try and solve the situation yourself. To wait on the Lord is to wait on His hand, His intervention—His guidance, His provision, His power, and His solution. Don't try and cobble together your destiny yourself. Don't try to force it into place. When it is God's time for you to fulfill your destiny, you will fulfill it perfectly. Rather than take matters into your own hands, leave them in God's. As the saying goes, "Let go. And let God."

James 5:7–8 talks about this a bit, although in a different context: "Therefore, brothers, be patient, until the Lord's coming. See how the farmer waits for the precious fruit of the earth and is patient with it until it receives the early and late rains. You also must be patient. Strengthen your hearts, because the Lord's coming is near." Just as a farmer must wait for the rains and the soil to produce the growth of the seed, we must also wait for the Lord to produce within us and through us the purpose He intends.

You have heard of the endurance of Job and how God rewarded his patience through giving him twice what he had before. The

Lord is full of compassion and mercy to those who will learn and practice the skill and art of waiting well. One of the ways you will know you have not yet perfected this art of waiting well is if you spend a lot of your time complaining.

A person who has a complaining spirit—someone who has a pattern of whining about a situation or about God—is not waiting well. Complaining reveals a lack of faith. Complaining reveals a heart seeking a solution more than the lesson on the journey to the solution. Now, instead of God being your deliverer, He must be your judge.

Never go outside of God to try and make happen what you are waiting on Him to make happen. Because when you do, you will only delay it happening. Scripture is replete with examples of people delaying the deliverance of their destiny because they tried to get there on their own. Abraham and Sarah had to wait twenty-five years before the promise of a child. The delay came because they went to the flesh to solve a situation of the spirit. Martha and Mary had to wait as Jesus intentionally delayed performing the miracle of raising their brother from the dead because their doubts, and subsequent faith, would be used to teach others for years to come.

Delays aren't always a cause for intervention. They are often a place to teach us something God wants us to learn or to receive something God wants us to receive first. Jesus told the disciples to go to Jerusalem and wait for the Holy Spirit before they went out to minister on His behalf. Hannah had to wait years before she got her first child. Ruth had to wait before she got her husband.

Part of the Christian experience, at various segments of our lives, is this one of waiting. Waiting on timing. Waiting on divine hookups. Waiting on preparation. Waiting on other people. Waiting on ourselves. Waiting on development. Waiting on . . . waiting.

Waiting on God means not going outside of God to resolve the issue.

It also means obeying God as you wait. Based on His revealed will from His Word, obey what you know. Because you will never see what God plans to do in secret unless He sees you obeying what He has already revealed. God never tells you everything He is going to do, but He has told you something. Whatever it is, obey that. However small, however insignificant it may seem—obey that. Do what you know to do even if you don't know what it is doing for you.

When you are sick, you go to the doctor, and if she finds an infection, she writes you a prescription. Guess what the doctor expects you to do in your pain while you are waiting to get better? Take medicine. She doesn't expect you to read about the medicine. She doesn't expect you to talk about the medicine. She doesn't even expect you to understand what the medicine is and how it works. Just take the medicine and let it work. Just do what the doctor told you to do and let the outcome present itself in time. When you or I take medicine, we wait for it to work. It is never instant.

But keep in mind, the longer you put off taking the medicine, the longer it will take for the medicine to work.

Far too many Christians like to talk to other people about what God's Word says. We like to think about it. Consider it. But very few will act on it.

Very few will live with the faith that tells us not to worry. Very few will forgive with a grace that tells us not to carry a grudge. Very few will go to a place we have never seen before, or leave the security of what we know for one where God is directing.

God, the Great Physician, has prescribed what we need in His Word. Whether or not we follow what He has revealed—things like love, forgiveness, trust, faith, hope, and more—will determine how long it takes for us to wait.

When did Job get God's reward and double blessing? After he prayed for his friends. After he showed grace and kindness to those who had brought him pain during his greatest moments of pain. Job followed the law of love and asked God to give goodness to others. When he did that, God gave goodness to Job.

> *Learning to wait well involves learning how to put into practice the everyday-ness of living as a child of God.*

Learning to wait well involves learning how to put into practice the everyday-ness of living as a child of God. It means putting into practice those things we already know. Forgiving. Loving. Believing. Working as unto the Lord, even if it's not your favorite place to work. Honoring the authority over you, even if you don't particularly like or respect him. Bearing one another's burdens, even when you feel weighed down by your own.

Do what God has already said to do.

Then watch Him usher you to your destiny.

My son Anthony came home from school one day with an assignment. This assignment involved planting a seed in a small pot, watering it, and watching it grow. It was an assignment for his science class. Anthony dutifully put his seed in the soil in the pot on Friday night then went about his normal play and evening business. When he woke up on Saturday, he ran to the window to look at the pot. Nothing had happened. Nothing had grown. Anthony came to me disappointed because the seed had yielded nothing overnight.

I had to explain to Anthony that this wasn't Jack's magic beans, which would grow into a vine reaching to the heavens overnight. This was a seed. And as with all seeds, it would take time to grow. It would require waiting, in faith. Watering, in faith. Watching, in faith.

This concept of waiting is very interesting when you break it down to its literal meaning. The concept in biblical times was used of strands that were plaited together, interwoven to make something bigger, brighter, and more whole. The word *wait* can refer to pulling together the strands of God's revealed will in an effort to tighten them up until something bigger is brought about through the combination of all things.

Waiting requires time. I'm sorry to have to stick with that truth. But it's true. So the sooner we accept it as true, the sooner we can learn to do it well.

Just like Anthony's seed beneath the soil, something was happening. It's not that nothing at all was taking place. It's just that nothing that Anthony could see was taking place. What was happening was occurring in secret underneath the dirt. And it would need to remain there until the right time it was to emerge.

When God is silent, He is not still. But a lot of His activity and a lot of His purposes are being woven underneath the dirt of our days. It is growing there out of our sight and in ways we cannot see—until such a time, within the confines of His purposes and His will, He is ready to reveal it.

Wait, my friend. Wait well.

Joseph's story ought to encourage you that it will one day be worth it.

Wait well.

CHAPTER SIXTEEN

The Path of Detours

 If anyone knew what it meant to wait without so much as hope on the horizon, it was Joseph. I don't need to rehash the events of his life here since we've covered them so thoroughly throughout these pages.

But by now, if you know anything at all about Joseph, you know this: Joseph spent the bulk of his life waiting on God to bring him into his destiny.

Joseph didn't even get to have his own family until he was well past the years that men in his culture wedded and had children. He didn't have a career with upward mobility either. After all, slavery and then a jail cell are usually pretty limited when it comes to promotion. Joseph held no degrees. He was an outsider in a culture, which was obsessed with their own culture. If anyone should have any reason to give up, throw in the towel, and just give in to a fatalistic mentality, it would be Joseph.

But Joseph didn't give in. He kept showing up, day in and day out. We know this because Scripture tells us that the Lord was with Joseph and also granted him favor with those around him. We also know that God continued to promote him wherever he was to have greater authority and influence.

> *Joseph spent the bulk of his life waiting on God to bring him into his destiny.*

Greater authority and influence doesn't go to the one who tosses in the towel. Great authority and influence usually goes to the one who is using that towel, and using it well. Even if it means all you can do with it is clean up someone else's mess. It's only a fairy tale, but it carries truth that resonates with all of us. Cinderella sang as she cleaned because once she had met the prince, she knew there was something bigger for her. It was just a matter of timing, which is how it always is with God. It's a matter of timing. It's a matter of Him setting up the intersections of life so that when you get there, the people you are connecting with are ready for you. And, even more importantly, you are ready to handle what has been given to you as well.

Joseph's waiting was a matter of timing. We read this in the book of Psalms, "He called down famine against the land and destroyed the entire food supply. He had sent a man ahead of them—Joseph, who was sold as a slave. They hurt his feet with shackles; his neck was put in an iron collar. Until the time his prediction came true, the word of the LORD tested him" (Ps. 105:16–19).

You'll notice an important set of words in that passage, "until the time." Joseph was afflicted. Joseph was a slave. Joseph was a prisoner. Joseph was broken, bound, and forgotten—from a human perspective. *Until the time.*

Until what time?

Until the time God was ready with all pieces of the puzzle to carry out His perfect plan in history.

One reason God has us waiting for various things and desires in our lives is because He is doing something bigger than you. It's bigger than you.

I know you are the one going through it, feeling it, experiencing it—being pained by it. But what He is doing *is* bigger than you. It's always bigger than you. Like the strands woven together to create a tapestry of an image no single strand has the ability to display, we are all interconnected through God in His divine plan. He is hooking things up.

You are one strand. Joseph was one strand in God's bigger kingdom plan of preserving a family for the building of a nation. Yes, Joseph was an important strand just as you are an important strand. But oftentimes the most important strands have to wait the longest and develop the most before being shown their part to play.

As you wait on your destiny, realize that one of the reasons you are waiting is because God is up to something bigger than just you. It involves time because there is more to deal with than just you.

Testing in Time

Everyone seems to want a blessing, but few want development. A kid will eat candy all day. They will take your money all day. But give them correction, discipline—guidance that goes against what they want—and they will often balk. Yet candy, games, and money aren't going to develop a child into becoming a productive adult. God knows the same holds true for us. In order for God to have Joseph fulfill his role as second-in-command in Egypt, He had to take him deeper first. He had to develop him first. He had to strengthen his humility, trust, confidence (as opposed to pride), and leadership skills. He also gave him lessons on dealing with accusers and haters along the way, since a position of prominence will no doubt attract the same.

It's like the army captain who had soldiers in training and he asked them all to jump over the riverbed. The goal was to get over the river and land on the other side. All of the men and women jumped, but none of them made it. Some made it halfway. Others made it two-thirds, but not one person made it over.

That's when the army captain let loose an alligator in the river and asked them to try again. This time, all of them made it. This is because sometimes you need some negative potential in your experience to take you further than you would go on your own. Sometimes you need to learn your lessons to pass the test. You need to experience the consequences of poor choices. You need to mature, focus, and eliminate outside distractions. You need to train your taste buds to not only know what is good but be willing to go without what is not. If Joseph had not experienced opulence and destitution as he had, he may not have handled the opulence he later obtained.

Sometimes you and I need to learn to trust God, worship Him, and wait for Him in spite of the reality that He is not providing anything for us right now in alignment with what we desire. It's easy to worship God and surrender to Him when all is well. It's not easy when you are in a jail, like Joseph.

And for you and me, that may be an emotional jail.

A relational jail—could be a relationship you wish you were never in but have no way out of—or a relationship you wish you had but are, at the moment, alone.

It could be a jail of finances or health or even your job. They call a job that gives you no purpose other than a paycheck wearing "velvet handcuffs" because you aren't as free as you really think you are.

Many of you either cooked or ate turkeys or hams over the holiday season. I would be in the "ate" category. Those of you who cook them know that they usually come with a temperature gauge of some sort that will pop up when the meat is ready. Or you stick in a thermometer to see what the temperature is inside the meat. The reason why this is necessary is because the appearance of meat can be deceiving. Meat can look cooked on the outside, but when you cut it open, it's still raw. It's nasty. It's got blood. It still has germs that can make you sick.

Christians are no different. Many of us can look put together and spiritual on the outside, but get to the heart of the matter, and you will discover that far too many are not nearly as spiritual as they give off. They are mean, nasty, and carry germs of bitterness, doubt, and ingratitude when you dig deep enough through difficult situations. Just because you say "hallelujah" to the message doesn't mean you are spiritual. Just because you preach the message doesn't mean you are spiritual either. God knows the state of each of our souls, and He won't pull us out of the oven of adversity and waiting until we are ready for what He has in store.

Waiting can be a way of life since spiritual growth and development usually take time. But there is a way to know that you are not alone while you are waiting on God. There is a way to know that "God is with you" just as He was with Joseph, and He is taking you to your destiny. We find this way in the book of Isaiah,

> Jacob, why do you say, and Israel, why do you assert: "My way is hidden from the LORD, and my claim is ignored by my God"? Do you not know? Have you not heard? Yahweh is the everlasting God, the creator of the whole earth. He never grows faint or weary; there is no limit to His understanding. He gives strength to the weary and strengthens the powerless. Youths may faint and grow weary, and young men stumble and fall, but those who trust in the LORD will renew their strength; they will soar on wings like eagles; they will run and not grow weary; they will walk and not faint. (Isa. 40:27–31)

Embedded in that verse is wisdom for how you will know God is with you on your detour. He has both a purpose and a plan for where you are right now, and—most importantly—so you will have perfected the art of "waiting well." When these things are in alignment, it says He will renew your strength.

He renews your strength.

If you have a smartphone, you will notice that you may begin the day at 100 percent battery charged, but as you go throughout the day, it moves down to 75 percent, and then 50 percent, and even 20 percent. If you do nothing about it, you'll eventually get a warning that you are low on your battery life. Things will shut down altogether if you don't quickly find a charger, or borrow one, and plug your smartphone in. Now, all of a sudden, what was almost out of strength starts to find new strength.

God says that one way you will know you are waiting well is He recharges you when you are running out of juice. One of the ways He does this is explained in verse 31: you "will soar on wings like eagles." There is an interesting reality about eagles that can apply as great insight to our spiritual lives if we will let it. When a mama eagle first builds her nest for her baby, she makes it comfortable. It's full of all the things the baby eagle needs to want to stay there. She feeds it. She warms it. She nurtures it.

But when it comes time for this baby eagle to fly, the mama eagle will begin to pull away the comfortable pieces of the nest. Bit by bit things are removed—exposing the growing eagle to a less ideal environment. Things begin to poke, prod, and annoy the young eagle. Eventually, after all the soft things have been taken away thus creating an irritation, she pushes the eagle out of the nest altogether.

First, she makes it so the eagle wouldn't mind leaving the nest because all of the comforts that were first known are now gone. Then she bumps the eagle right on out, forcing it to flap its wings. The problem comes because the young eagle has never flown before, and doesn't know how to fly. And getting it right on the first try isn't likely. So what does the mama eagle do? As her young eagle continues to flap and fall and flap and fall, she swoops down to it and catches it with her talons and often with her wings. Then she delivers the young eagle back up to the nest until it's time to try again.

Friend, you may feel like you are falling, but God is just teaching you how to fly. You may feel like you are about to crash into the rocks at the bottom of the canyon, but God has His eyes on you, and He will swoop down out of nowhere and catch you with His grace. It's called divine intervention, and He is a master at it. This is when God comes out of nowhere, brings something into your life that catches you when you thought you were going to quit, lose your mind, give up—and He catches you. He doesn't change it. But He lets you know He's there.

Another way you know God is renewing your strength is in the part of the passage that says "they will run and not grow weary." This is when God supernaturally gives you a second wind. This is when you get to that place that you can't go past, you can't go on, you are huffing and puffing, and all of a sudden you get what run-ners call "the second wind." It's new strength. God doesn't swoop down and lift you out of it this time, but He gives you the strength to keep going on while in it. Sometimes that comes through a ser-mon or a book. Sometimes it comes through a song. Sometimes it comes through an encouraging word from a friend or an inspira-tional post on social media. It can come through any number of things, but—whatever it is—God uses it to give you strength just when you need it the most. You now have the ability and energy to keep going.

Then there are those times when God doesn't swoop down and carry you on His wings; He doesn't give you a second wind, but He keeps you from getting weary when you walk. This is when God doesn't change the situation; He just changes you in it. You can still go on, even if that means going fairly slow, like me at the annual Turkey Trot.

The Turkey Trot takes place in Dallas every year around Thanksgiving, and the point of the event is to exercise, by running, before the big feast. But since I had orthoscopic surgery on my knee some time ago, and since I still get arthritis in it, I cannot run. If I run, the pounding will cause my knee to swell. I used to run ten miles a day, but now I can't even run one mile. While many people are trotting at the Turkey Trot, I walk. And, funny enough, I'm not the only one walking. There's usually a group of us who wind up walking the trot. And when you walk with others, you sometimes forget you are walking at all. You start talking. You start laughing.

You look at the nature surrounding you, and before you know it, you have reached your destination. I don't recall ever getting weary while walking the Turkey Trot. God has a way of doing that if we will just keep going—He will bring people alongside of us to help us along.

At the airport they have what are called moving sidewalks. These are places for people with a lot of luggage to step on and take a rest. Stand to the right if you want a rest, or walk on the left if you want the moving sidewalk to get you there even faster. Either way, the moving sidewalk will get you to your destination.

Friend, God has a number of ways for you to wait on Him. Sometimes that involves a time of rest. Other times it involves being pushed from the nest. Whatever the case, when you wait well, He will be there to see you to the end.

And, frankly, the end just might surprise you.

No Place like Home

One of my favorite stories is the one of Dorothy from Kansas. You've heard it. You've probably seen it. Or maybe you've even seen the recent Broadway musical called *Wicked*. However the styles of songs or clothing may be, based on the version you love best, the story remains the same throughout. A young girl named Dorothy, along with her faithful dog Toto, are feeling discontent. They are feeling like there must be more to life than what they are living. Dorothy longs to go to another place where she feels she will have the chance to live out the reason why she is here. In short, she's searching for her destiny. Where she belongs. Where she should wind up in this life.

Dorothy's discontentment sets her off on a path, just like much of our discontentment does for us. It nudges us, pushes us, and prods us in the direction of seeking. We find ourselves on a yellow brick road of questions, discoveries, and even detours. Along Dorothy's yellow-brick-road experience, she meets some others who are looking for that thing that is missing in them.

Maybe it's the courage to live out who they were created to be.

Or the skills and training to reach their full potential intellectually.

Or maybe it's someone who needs softening, to develop compassion and a bigger heart for others.

Whatever the need, Dorothy links up with others in a quest for destiny.

But just as God never takes someone from A to Z in a straight line, Dorothy and her friends didn't get to where they needed to go either without first going through some detours and distractions. There was the poppy field, which sought to lull them to sleep in the ease of wonderment. Then there were also the monkeys sent to target and frighten them into turning back.

But the greatest problem of all was the wicked witch, Elphaba, who did everything she could to stop them, just as Satan does everything he can to stop us from moving forward to reach our destiny. All along the path Dorothy and her friends faced difficulty after difficulty. But the key in getting to their destination is they never gave up. They had a guiding force named Glenda overseeing their progress toward their destiny, similar to how you and I have the Holy Spirit guiding us in the right direction. Because of this, they pushed through, ultimately making it to the wizard—the one to give them what they lacked.

The irony of the story is that once they reached the wizard, they realized he had nothing to give. He was smoke and mirrors, after all—a man in search of his own true realization of destiny himself.

But they also came to grasp that the fulfillment of their own greatest desires were a lot closer than they ever thought. They were right there within each of them all along, just needing to be cultivated and developed on the way. Which is where our destinies usually are—within us in seed form, needing the time to be nurtured. In their search for destiny on the detours of the yellow brick road, they had grown and matured to the point where they could now live theirs out. The lion found his courage. The scarecrow found his brain. The tin man found his heart.

Yet Dorothy found the greatest lesson of them all.

She discovered that sometimes where you are trying to go isn't any better than where you are.

When you truly come to realize this—along with the value of who you are and the worth of those around you—you discover your destiny. In recognizing how your life sovereignly merges and intersects with others at God's divinely right time—each day, every day—you not only bring Him glory, but you also bring benefit, purpose, and joy to yourself and to all.

Click your heels three times, my friend.

Go ahead.

You are closer than you think.

Conclusion

 Not too long ago I had the privilege and honor to travel to South Africa for a week of teaching. While there, I toured several historic sites. Nothing touched me more than learning firsthand about the life of the great man Nelson Mandela. Seeing how he was impacted, what he overcame, and the circumstances in which he somehow not only managed to survive but also to develop into the man he became was a humbling experience for me.

Nelson Mandela lived these lessons of detours unlike anyone else in modern times. Who would have imagined he would go from prisoner to the presidency?

Who would have thought that a twenty-seven-year detour in a prison for nothing more than the color of his skin and the hope of his heart would one day lead to a revolution of freedom from an evil system of apartheid?

Who would have looked at him as the small, poor child he once was and seen one of the most influential worldwide leaders of all time?

Few, if any.

Nelson Mandela's words ring profound, reflecting thoughts—fine-tuned and tested by the harshest realities of life. But something he once said settled deep in my soul the first time I read it, and especially as I stood on the soil of this man's homeland. Nelson Mandela said, "For to be free is not merely to cast off one's chains, but to live in a way that respects and enhances the freedom of others."

> *"For to be free is not merely to cast off one's chains, but to live in a way that respects and enhances the freedom of others." —Nelson Mandela*

This quote is exactly what Nelson Mandela spent the latter years of his life doing, at a pace and fervency unlike few others. His name will forever live as one of the greatest men of history because he allowed his destiny to be a place of deliverance for people other than himself.

We've gone on a journey through the pages of this book with another man who once languished in prison. We've traced the footsteps of another prisoner turned prince in the palace. Who would have thought that the forgotten slave boy in the pit and prison would one day become the second-in-command in a foreign nation? No one would have predicted Joseph's future.

Few, if any.

But God did.

God knew.

God had a plan for this man.

What about you? It's your turn. Would anyone look at your life and say, "There is a person destined for greatness"? Do the walls of your home and your heart resemble a life of purpose? Or are you—like Joseph and Nelson Mandela—in a place right now where hope seems distant and light seems smothered by darkness? Are you in a place you never planned to go? With people you never planned to know? Situations you never thought you would be in? Have you made mistakes you regret and never thought you could ever make?

If that's you, do not lose heart. Because the sovereign, providential hand of God can and will use all of it to usher you to your destiny, when you allow Him. As long as you choose to live with a small god in your perspective, the circumstances of life will dictate your detours. But the moment you expand the meaning of God to this all-encompassing sovereign deity where nothing gets to you unless it passes through His fingers first, you will see Him move.

Yes, you may not enjoy the prison or the pit. But God has a plan for all of it. He has a blueprint in heaven with your name on it. And this blueprint, this roadmap, is all designed to bring you to your destiny.

You have a destiny. You have a divine design for your life. It may be a little foggy right now. It may not have been totally manifested for any number of reasons. But, nevertheless, you have a destiny and a purpose where God desires to take you.

Detours develop your character.

Tests strengthen your spiritual aptitude.

And delays allow God to prepare the people you are to impact so that they are ready when you connect.

Remember, your destiny is never only about you. Your destiny always involves you benefiting others beyond yourself.

So many believers want God to bless them. And there is nothing wrong with wanting a blessing. But far too few truly understand what the definition of a blessing is. A blessing can be defined as experiencing, enjoying, and extending the goodness of God in your life. It is not merely something God does to you but also something He does through you. James reminds us that true religion manifests itself in ministry to others (James 1:27). True religion never involves only you. God is always doing more than one thing at a time—it involves you, yes, but it's not only about you. It's about advancing God's kingdom agenda.

And because your destiny is not only about you, sometimes your detours and delays are not specifically tied to you. They are tied to the people or situations that need to be ready for you. God influences different things in different places at different times so that they will be ready when He creates the hookup. He is doing something elsewhere that you do not even know about so that the something elsewhere will be ready when it's time for you to connect.

Joseph sat in jail for two long years until the cupbearer remembered him. But it wasn't the right time for the cupbearer to remember him earlier. It was only the right time when Pharaoh was ready, the nation was ready, the situation was ready, and the cupbearer was ready. Joseph didn't sit in the prison those two years due to any fault of his own. He was there because God was arranging circumstances beyond and outside of him that would need him. But those circumstances and people beyond and outside of him wouldn't know that they needed him for two full years.

Here is what I don't want you to miss from this example of Joseph and his destiny: Joseph had absolutely no idea about Pharaoh's dream. He had never met Pharaoh. He probably had never even thought he would one day meet Pharaoh. Joseph doesn't know what is going on in the world outside of him. He is in a hole all by himself. But in less than twenty-four hours, his world changes. In twenty-four hours he's given a shave, given new clothes, released from prison, and standing before the most powerful man on the planet.

Not only that, Joseph is promoted to a place of prominence and authority. In one of the most bizarre twists of "fate" in all time, we read,

> Then Pharaoh said to his servants, "Can we find a man like this, in whom is a divine spirit?" So Pharaoh said to Joseph, "Since God has informed you of all this, there is no one so discerning and wise as you are. You shall be over my house, and according to your command all my people shall

do homage; only in the throne I will be greater than you." Pharaoh said to Joseph, "See, I have set you over all the land of Egypt." Then Pharaoh took off his signet ring from his hand and put it on Joseph's hand, and clothed him in garments of fine linen and put the gold necklace around his neck. He had him ride in his second chariot; and they proclaimed before him, "Bow the knee!" And he set him over all the land of Egypt. (Gen. 41:38–43 NASB)

Joseph was set over all the land of Egypt! Why? Because Pharaoh said that man had a special spirit. "Can we find a man like this, in whom is a divine spirit?" Pharaoh asked his counsel. It was a rhetorical question, seeing as it came from Pharaoh. But it has been recorded for us in Scripture so that we may see an example of God's mighty hand in moving someone from the dungeon to destiny. Joseph didn't muscle his way in. He didn't climb any corporate ladder. He fulfilled what God has said in His Word, "'Not by strength or by might, but by My Spirit,' says the LORD of Hosts" (Zech. 4:6).

The Spirit can do an awful lot in twenty-four hours.

Friend, when God is ready to move, it doesn't take long. When He is ready to change your situation because you have allowed Him to develop you spiritually, He can do it suddenly. Out of nowhere. Immediately. Like a shooting star across the sky, God can bring something from nothing to brighten your night. So don't get upset when you can't see any movement in your dungeon, because God is working elsewhere to prepare the place, the person, or the people for where He is taking you.

When God changes your status in life and He removes you from a negative situation—or changes you in it—keep your eyes open for the blessing He wants you to be.

This is a pattern I found in my research on Joseph that showed up throughout Scripture in many people's stories. God would take a person on detours only to later do something in their life to turn their situation around and use them to benefit others outside of themselves.

God told Abraham in Genesis 12 that He wanted him to leave the land of his parents and go to a land that He would show him. But He wasn't going to show Abraham in advance. Abraham had to go in faith. Now, if you study Abraham's life, you will see that he goes through twenty-five years of detours. Twenty-five years of good, bad, and ugly occur before God sets things up for his blessing. In that time, Abraham matured through tests and trials, and his faith deepened. He made mistakes. Some of them were fairly large mistakes with lasting repercussions. But ultimately Abraham was ready for the blessing and destiny God had told him about so many decades before.

Another time a pattern like this happened in Scripture is found in the book of Exodus. Bear in mind that when the Bible was penned, there were no chapter and verse divisions. Scholars added those divisions later so that places could be located quickly. In Exodus 2:23–25 it describes a critical situation, "After a long time, the king of Egypt died. The Israelites groaned because of their difficult labor, and they cried out; and their cry for help ascended to God because of the difficult labor. So God heard their groaning, and He remembered His covenant with Abraham, Isaac, and Jacob. God saw the Israelites, and He took notice."

Israel is crying out. The Israelites are seeking deliverance. And God says, essentially, "I hear you, I hear you." As we move to chapter 3, we jump to an entirely different location. We jump to something that may seem completely irrelevant to what we just read. But remember—there were no chapter and verse divisions in the original story. The writer just left off from the children of Israel crying out for deliverance in Egypt and jumped all the way over to Moses in a desert: "Meanwhile Moses was shepherding the flock of his father-in-law Jethro, the priest of Midian. He led the flock to the far side of the wilderness and came to Horeb, the mountain of God" (3:1).

Moses has been leading sheep in the middle of nowhere for forty years. What does Moses have to do with an entire nation of people crying out to God for deliverance? Everything. Because during those forty years in the desert, Moses had been learning lessons in obedience, lessons in patience, lessons in humility, lessons in shepherding, lessons in traversing and surviving a desert, and more.

And forty years prior, the Israelites were not to the point of crying out for a leader either. If you recall the story, Moses had tried to present himself as their deliverer back then, but they did not have eyes to see or ears to hear. They were not yet broken to the point that they needed someone like him to intervene. God was waiting for both sides of the situation to be ready before ushering Moses into his destiny and kingdom purpose through the moment at the burning bush.

Here is another time this pattern occurred. You remember Esther? The pretty girl and shining star? After all, her name means "star." Esther has gone from the slums to the palace. She is a queen now. A queen with a part to play in the deliverance of an entire nation of people. When an evil plot arises to destroy her people, Esther bravely responds with the courage to address the situation before her king. Yes, at first she wavered, but the ultimate sign of courage is not that fears exist but rather that you push past them.

At just the right moment in time, Esther's destiny coincided with the destinies of her people—delivering them from certain death by giving them the opportunity to defend themselves against a sinister scheme.

Your destiny and kingdom purpose often involve both a hookup and a hope to people beyond yourself. Look for both as God guides you. Pray for both as you wait patiently. Sharpen your faith, hone your skills, seek His face, and He will move you from detour to destiny.

Keep your eyes wide open, okay?

Because God has a way of ushering you to your destiny—*suddenly*.

The Urban Alternative

The Urban Alternative (TUA) equips, empowers, and unites Christians to impact *individuals, families, churches,* and *communities* through a thoroughly kingdom agenda worldview. In teaching truth, we seek to transform lives.

The core cause of the problems we face in our personal lives, homes, churches, and societies is a spiritual one; therefore, the only way to address it is spiritually. We've tried a political, social, economic, and even a religious agenda.

It's time for a **kingdom agenda**.

The kingdom agenda can be defined as the visible manifestation of the comprehensive rule of God over every area of life.

The unifying central theme throughout the Bible is the glory of God and the advancement of His kingdom. The conjoining thread from Genesis to Revelation—from beginning to end—is focused on one thing: God's glory through advancing God's kingdom.

When you do not have that theme, the Bible becomes disconnected stories that are great for inspiration but seem to be unrelated in purpose and direction. The Bible exists to share God's movement in history toward the establishment and expansion of His kingdom highlighting the connectivity throughout, which is the kingdom. Understanding that increases the relevancy of this several thousand-year-old manuscript to your day-to-day living because the kingdom is not only then; it is now.

The absence of the kingdom's influence in our personal and family lives, churches, and communities has led to a deterioration in our world of immense proportions:

- People live segmented, compartmentalized lives because they lack God's kingdom worldview.
- Families disintegrate because they exist for their own satisfaction rather than for the kingdom.
- Churches are limited in the scope of their impact because they fail to comprehend that the goal of the church is not the church itself but the kingdom.
- Communities have nowhere to turn to find real solutions for real people who have real problems because the church has become divided, ingrown, and unable to transform the cultural landscape in any relevant way.

The kingdom agenda offers us a way to see and live life with a solid hope by optimizing the solutions of heaven. When God, and His rule, is no longer the final and authoritative standard under which all else falls, order and hope leaves with Him. But the reverse of that is true as well: As long as you have God, you have hope. If God is still in the picture, and as long as His agenda is still on the table, it's not over.

Even if relationships collapse, God will sustain you. Even if finances dwindle, God will keep you. Even if dreams die, God will revive you. As long as God, and His rule, is still the overarching rule in your life, family, church, and community, there is always hope.

Our world needs the King's agenda. Our churches need the King's agenda. Our families need the King's agenda.

In many major cities there is a loop drivers can take when they want to get somewhere on the other side of the city but don't necessarily want to head straight through downtown. This loop will take you close enough to the city so you can see its towering buildings and skyline but not close enough to actually experience it.

This is precisely what we, as a culture, have done with God. We have put Him on the "loop" of our personal, family, church, and community lives. He's close enough to be at hand should we need Him in an emergency but far enough away that He can't be the center of who we are.

We want God on the "loop," not the King of the Bible who comes downtown into the very heart of our ways. Leaving God on the "loop" brings about dire consequences as we have seen in our own lives and with others. But when we make God, and His rule, the centerpiece of all we think, do, or say, it is then that we will experience Him in the way He longs to be experienced by us.

He wants us to be kingdom people with kingdom minds set on fulfilling His kingdom's purposes. He wants us to pray, as Jesus did, "Not my will, but Thy will be done." Because His is the kingdom, the power, and the glory.

There is only one God, and we are not Him. As King and Creator, God calls the shots. It is only when we align ourselves underneath His comprehensive hand that we will access His full power and authority in all spheres of life: personal, familial, church, and community.

As we learn how to govern ourselves under God, we then transform the institutions of family, church, and society from a biblically based kingdom worldview.

Under Him, we touch heaven and change Earth.

To achieve our goal we use a variety of strategies, approaches, and resources for reaching and equipping as many people as possible.

Broadcast Media

Millions of individuals experience *The Alternative with Dr. Tony Evans* through the daily radio broadcast playing on nearly **one thousand RADIO outlets** and in more than **one hundred countries**. The broadcast can also be seen on several television networks and is viewable online at TonyEvans.org. You can also listen or view the daily broadcast by downloading the Tony Evans app for free in the App store. More than four million message downloads occur each year.

Leadership Training

The Tony Evans Training Center (TETC) facilitates educational programming that embodies the ministry philosophy of Dr. Tony Evans as expressed through the kingdom agenda. The training courses focus on leadership development and discipleship in the following five tracks:

- Bible and Theology
- Personal Growth
- Family and Relationships
- Church Health and Leadership Development
- Society and Community Impact Strategies

The TETC program includes courses for both local and online students. Furthermore, TETC programming includes course work for nonstudent attendees. Pastors, Christian leaders, and Christian laity, both local and at a distance, can seek out The Kingdom Agenda Certificate for personal, spiritual, and professional development. Some courses are valued for CEU credit as well as viable in transferring for college credit with our partner school(s).

The Kingdom Agenda Pastors (KAP) provides a *viable network* for *like-minded pastors* who embrace the Kingdom Agenda philosophy. Pastors have the opportunity to go deeper with Dr. Tony Evans as they are given greater biblical knowledge, practical applications, and resources to impact individuals, families, churches, and communities. KAP welcomes *senior and associate pastors* of all churches. KAP also offers an annual Summit held each year in Dallas with intensive seminars, workshops, and resources.

Pastors' Wives Ministry, founded by Dr. Lois Evans, provides *counsel, encouragement,* and *spiritual resources* for pastors' wives as they serve with their husbands in the ministry. A primary focus of the ministry is the KAP Summit that offers senior pastors' wives a safe place to *reflect, renew,* and *relax* along with training in personal development, spiritual growth, and care for their emotional and physical well-being.

Community Impact

National Church Adopt-A-School Initiative (NCAASI) prepares churches across the country to impact communities by using *public schools as the primary vehicle for effecting positive social change* in urban youth and families. Leaders of churches, school districts, faith-based organizations, and other nonprofit organizations are equipped with the knowledge and tools to *forge partnerships* and build *strong social service delivery systems*. This training is based on the comprehensive church-based community impact strategy conducted by Oak Cliff Bible Fellowship. It addresses such areas as economic development, education, housing, health revitalization, family renewal, and racial reconciliation. We assist churches in tailoring the model to meet specific needs of their communities while simultaneously addressing the spiritual and moral frame of reference. Training events are held annually in the Dallas area at Oak Cliff Bible Fellowship.

Athlete's Impact (AI) exists as an outreach both into and through the sports arena. Coaches are the most influential factor in young people's lives, even ahead of their parents. With the growing rise of fatherlessness in our culture, more young people are looking to their coaches for guidance, character development, practical needs, and hope. After coaches on the influencer scale fall athletes. Athletes (whether professional or amateur) influence younger athletes and kids within their spheres of impact. Knowing this, we have made it our aim to equip and train coaches and athletes on how to live out and utilize their God-given roles for the benefit of the kingdom. We aim to do this through our iCoach App, weCoach Football Conference as well as resources such as *The Playbook: A Life Strategy Guide for Athletes.*

Resource Development

We are fostering lifelong learning partnerships with the people we serve by providing a variety of published materials. Dr. Evans has published more than one hundred unique titles based on more than forty years of preaching whether that is in booklet, book, or Bible study format. The goal is to strengthen individuals in their walk with God and service to others.

For more information, and a complimentary copy of Dr. Evans' devotional newsletter, call (800) 800-3222 *or* write TUA at P.O. Box 4000, Dallas, TX, 75208, *or* visit us online at www.TonyEvans.org.

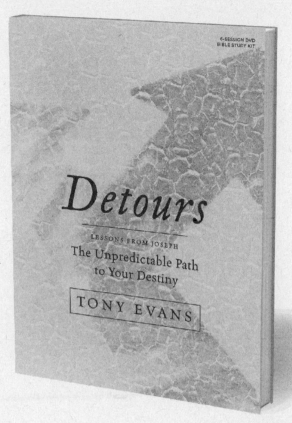

Do you know others
WHO HAVE HAD A FEW DETOURS?

This message from Tony Evans is too good to keep to yourself. Fortunately, it's easy to share with your small group (or just a group of friends). The *Detours* Bible study includes step-by-step plans for six group sessions, leader tips, a promotional video you can use to invite people, 25- to 30-minute teaching videos featuring author Tony Evans, and more.